The VDI Delusion

Brian Madden
Gabe Knuth
Jack Madden

The VDI Delusion

Why desktop virtualization failed to live up to the hype, and what the future enterprise desktop will really look like.

Copyright © 2012 Brian Madden, Gabe Knuth, & Jack Madden

Published by
Burning Troll Productions, LLC
San Francisco, California
www.brianmadden.com/books

Written by
Brian Madden
Gabe Knuth
Jack Madden

Illustrations & Cover Design
Rick Barnes

Copy Editor
Monica Sambataro

ISBN 978-0-9852174-0-2 (hard cover) 978-0-9852174-1-9 (eBook)

Set in Chaparral Light

Second Printing, November 2012

Printed in the United States of America

Contents

From the Authors

From Brian Madden:

I've spent the past sixteen years preparing to write this book—fourteen working alongside Gabe, and eight with Jack. Thanks to them—and everyone—who've put up with me that whole time and have now given me the opportunity to put all my soapbox issues into one single book. Also, thanks to TechTarget for not making me live in Boston and for not firing me because I brought my own laptop and use Dropbox.

And of course, thanks to Gabe and Jack for agreeing to write this book with me. This was truly a collaboration. Those two kept me on track, wrote a bunch of stuff that I couldn't, and helped to shape and structure 60,000 random words into a pretty good story. O-H!

From Gabe Knuth:

I-O! I spent many years as a consultant, first in Cleveland, where I grew up, and later in Omaha, where I live now. In 2007, I ditched the 9 to 5 to become a professional blogger, which wasn't really a type of job at the time. I wasn't much of a writer in school, so if you see any of my old teachers, show them this book and tell them you don't have to be a good writer as long as you have a good copy editor.

My thanks to Brian for including me in this book and everything else he's done for me in the past fifteen years; to my wife Kaylene, son Carson, and daughter Elizabeth, all of whom I am so fortunate to be around all day, every day. And thanks to Energizer for making the AAA batteries that power my noise-canceling headphones that I use to escape the constant sound coming from wherever the kids happen to be playing.

From Jack Madden:

I'm the guy who writes most of the stuff at ConsumerizeIT. com. I've been doing all sorts of things with Brian and Gabe for eight years now, and working with them is awesome. Thanks, guys! I also especially want to thank the BriForum gang—I can't emphasize enough how much of an inspiration all of you have been to me. Finally, thank you to Kevin Goodman for his help with this book.

Foreword

I FIRST MET BRIAN MADDEN IN 2002 at the Citrix iForum conference in Orlando. Brian was working for HP, and he asked me what I thought of his idea to leave HP to start his own company writing for BrianMadden.com full time.

At the time, I was the founder and VP of development for KevSoft Corporation as well as the author of two Windows programming books, a dozen or so articles for various programming journals, and a couple of patents. I looked at this kid (Brian was in his early twenties, but looked sixteen) and could tell that he had already made up his mind and was just looking to me for confirmation. "I think it's a great idea," I said with all the conviction I could muster.

As it turned out, I was right. BrianMadden.com became the definitive location for peer support, news, and information on all things Citrix and Terminal Server, and every book Brian wrote became a best seller in its category.

In his usual "in-your-face" style, Brian's blog posts told users exactly what he thought about a particular product or company. Of course not all the reviews were flattering, and this would often lead to consternation among vendors. I remember when one vendor in particular cornered me at Citrix iForum Edinburgh with a conversation that went something like this:

Vendor: I heard Brian is actually on the Citrix payroll.
Me: Do you even read his blog? No way.
Vendor: I heard he's never even installed Citrix.
Me: Seriously. Have you ever met him? If so, it would be clear that he knows his stuff.
Vendor: He has blue hair.

Me: Okay now I know you don't know Brian! (Mainly because blue was his hair color last year. Now it's bright red.)

In 2005, KevSoft changed its name to RTO Software and for some reason promoted me to CEO. This change led to a big regret I have had in my professional career: Since I was busy transitioning roles, I did not submit a session for Brian's first BriForum conference in Washington, D.C that April. Brian conceived BriForum as a vendor-neutral conference to counterbalance iForum. Brian gathered top industry experts such as Dr. Bernhard (Benny) Tritsch, Ron Oglesby, Tim Mangan, Jeroen van de Kamp, and others to present on a variety of topics, with Brian being the keynote and one of the main speakers. The event was a hit, and last year Brian and his team celebrated their tenth BriForum. As gratitude for the speakers who presented at all ten BriForums, Brian created bobblehead dolls of Benny, Ron, Tim and Jeroen! So while I've presented every BriForum since, missing that first BriForum meant that I missed my chance at immortality as a bobblehead. Aaargh!

When Brian started BrianMadden.com and BriForum, the industry was primarily focused on Citrix server-based computing technologies. Although a few vendors had products that allowed users to remotely access regular desktops as early as 2000, Jerry Chen of VMware is generally credited with coining the term "VDI" which led to the redefinition of an entire industry.

In 2010, VMware acquired my company (RTO Software) to strengthen their foray into the VDI market, and I suddenly found myself in the center of the action as a part of the product management team for VMware's VDI product, View. Never being a big fan of VDI, I caused quite a stir in my first off-site strategy meeting when I suggested that VDI in general and View in particular were best suited for niche use cases. I wonder how many of my colleagues shared my opinion: At last count, all but one of the original RTO employees VMware had acquired had either left VMware or had been transferred off of the VDI product line. I'm sure each individual had his or her own reasons for moving on, but by the time I left VMware in February 2012, every position between me and the CEO, Paul Maritz, had changed over twice. And Jerry Chen, the original force behind VDI? He had transferred away from the VDI team before I even got there.

In a conversation I had with Brian just prior to my leaving VMware, I lamented that I was tired of pushing the premise of VDI when in fact it was no better feature-wise, in my opinion, than a ten-year-old desktop PC. That's when Brian shared that he, Gabe, and Jack were writing a comprehensive and critical analysis book about the VDI delusion that is taking place. In a very clear and often humorous way, they have laid out in this book why they believe that the promise of VDI is much more alluring than the reality of what can be delivered today. This book also lays out a grand vision for the future of desktop computing, and I hope you read it prior to formulating any strategy for delivering applications and data to your users.

—Kevin Goodman

Introduction: The Demise of the Desktop, the Rise of the Workspace

Note from Brian Madden: This book is being brought to you for free thanks to Stoneware. They did not write the book, rather, they bought enough copies so that you could have it without paying for it. Thanks to them for that!

By Rick German, CEO of Stoneware

If you've picked up this book, you're probably looking for some key insights into why VDI has failed to deliver what it promised. Many other people wonder the same thing too, which is why it's exciting to see Brian, Gabe, and Jack take on the challenge of showing us exactly why there is a VDI Delusion.

In order to understand why IT has moved towards VDI, we need to look at the circumstances. IT finds itself in the midst of one of the biggest sea changes since the transformation from the mainframe to the personal computer. The way IT services are delivered, the devices accessing those services, and the means by which these devices are managed will be dramatically different from the traditional methods utilized over the last fifteen years.

Today, many organizations find themselves struggling to adapt to a rapidly changing computing environment. While the challenges are numerous, they can be broadly categorized into three select areas: service, devices, and management.

Services: How we deliver services to end users is rapidly changing. With the evolution of the Internet and web technologies such as HTML5, more and more applications are being deployed within an organization's private data center and as hosted services across the Internet. To make matters more complicated, there are still large numbers of applications that remain on local devices which are unlikely to be moved to private data centers or public clouds.

Devices: The device market is dramatically changing from what we knew even five years ago. The introduction of netbooks, smart phones, and tablets has created new challenges for IT in terms of capabilities, capacities, connectivity, operating systems, and management. IT finds itself in a new era computing where it must deliver many of the same services across a much more diverse set of computing devices.

Management: This new device market, along with web technologies, is redefining the term "personal computing." For the first time, a user's personal and professional computing life is merging into one. A user who purchased a tablet wants desperately to use it for both work and personal needs. An increasing number of these devices are not owned or managed by IT. Traditional desktop management finds itself unable to address the growing phenomena of users bringing their own technology to perform work-related tasks.

IT now finds itself in the perfect storm. Devices, the delivery of services, and management of the overall IT environment is in a great state of flux. New platforms and technologies will evolve to address the needs of both IT and the end user.

Many IT departments chose to pursue VDI as a way to solve these challenges. End users want access to files, applications, and data from anywhere and from any device in the simplest way possible.

In the chapters to come, you will learn why VDI is not the end-all be-all it was promoted to be in the last decade. Brian, Gabe, and Jack have stated a compelling case as to why the hype has been greater than the reality. While effective in some niches, VDI is just too expensive, and ultimately inflexible to comprehend the new reality of consumerization.

We hope you enjoy the book as we will build on the premise above in Chapter 13 and discuss potential solutions to the VDI dilemma.

Chapter 1

Why Are We Here?

IF YOU'VE PICKED UP THIS BOOK, you know that desktop virtualization and VDI (virtual desktop infrastructure) are all the rage right now. This is understandable given that the topic of virtualization in general is hot right now, and everyone's trying to figure out what their desktop strategy is going to be now that Macs, tablets, and the cloud are gaining popularity.

So why not virtualize your desktops? Why not build VDI and convert your desktops to virtual machines (VMs) that run in your data center or the cloud with users connecting remotely? Why not put hypervisors on your users' laptops so you can manage a bunch of VM desktops instead of managing physical desktops?

The technology to do all this became generally available years ago, yet desktop virtualization and VDI are far from mainstream. Sure, there are pockets of success here and there, but a major revolution? Hardly! In fact, it seems like the only people who are really talking about it are the ones who are trying to sell it to you!

The whole desktop virtualization and VDI thing reminds us of when we were in high school and heard rumors about what sex was like. Back then we had this vague notion that something great was out there. We weren't doing it ourselves, but other kids said they were and we thought they were cool. But we also wondered, were they *really* doing it? Or were they just saying they were to sound cool?

Of course some kids actually were having sex, but because they were so inexperienced, did they actually know if they were doing it right? For many of them, it seemed awkward and weird. Is this really what it's supposed to be like? Years later it got better, and we looked back and laughed at how naive we were then. But what did we know at the time? We were just getting started. It was all new and exciting.

This is where most of us are today with desktop virtualization. Everyone is talking about it, but who's actually doing it? Are the ones who are doing it doing it right? Should we all be doing it?

We all heard the analysts and consultants tell us that 2009 was supposed to be the "year of VDI." Then it was 2010, then 2011. There are probably people out there now saying that *next* year will be the year. But if VDI hasn't taken off yet, why not? Is the technology not ready? Are people too stupid to do it right? What's the problem?

We're going to spend the rest of this book trying to answer those questions. Then we'll try to provide some direction for what you can do instead, since clearly VDI is not taking over the world anytime soon. The first step to understanding VDI is to look at how companies think about desktops in general these days.

The Current State of the Enterprise Desktop

For most IT departments today, the desktop is no more strategic than the desk lamp or the office chair. It's something that's needed, for sure, but it's seen as more of a necessary evil rather than something that can be strategic and make one company stand out from another. Most IT professionals prefer to spend as little time as possible thinking about the desktop, instead focusing on cool things like software as a service (SaaS) and the cloud.

Even at large companies with dedicated desktop teams, many of the people on those teams view their desktop duties merely as a stepping-stone toward a "real" career working with servers. Their desktop role is a temporary position to be tolerated on their way to greatness, much like politicians who must endure years of local politics before they can run for national office.

So it comes as no surprise that when we ask companies to explain their desktop strategy to us, many desktop engineers simply shrug and vaguely point to a shipping pallet full of brown cardboard boxes with HP or Dell labels on them. Their "strategy" is that they order midlevel desktops and laptops by the pallet. Some of the more enterprising folks work with their vendors to have the perfect image preloaded onto the machines at the factory, but those of us who've been in the business awhile know that those images are out of date no matter how fast the shipping time is. So instead, they have a bunch of interns who unpack the new hardware, load the corporate image on them, configure each one for the right user, deliver it, and cross their fingers. This whole process is repeated ad infinitum until they get promoted out of the desktop group.

This "new desktop built by IT every four years" cycle has been going on for decades without much thought, and that was fine. But then a few years ago people started pushing this desktop virtualization concept by telling desktop admins that everything they've been doing for the past twenty years is inefficient. "It's a crazy endless cycle," they'd say. "You need to break free of the hamster wheel of never-ending buy-configure-deploy-maintain-fix-repeat!"

The thing is, those of us involved in this four-year desktop cycle don't actually think it's so bad. Sure, *in theory* there might be a better way. But we've been doing the same thing for twenty years. Heck, we've been doing the same thing with Windows XP for ten years. (We even know the XP product key by heart!) So we're pretty good at this whole cycle, even if it is the "old" way. What's wrong with that?

We'll tell you what's wrong with it: *Nothing!* There is nothing wrong with this scenario! Frankly, most of us would be happy for it to continue another fifteen years. This brings us to Fact No. 1 of this book—VDI vendors are not competing against each other. They're competing against the status quo. They're competing against those pallets full of Dells that you've been buying for the past twenty years.

Now as it happens, the desktop industry *has* been on the verge of a transformation for the past few years. Do you know what that transformation is? If you answered "desktop virtualization," you'd be...*wrong!*

The big thing that everyone in the desktop world has been focusing on recently is not desktop virtualization—it's Windows 7. Even two or three years ago, we all knew we were going to go to Windows 7. But since the world at large was (and is) still on Windows XP, we had to deal with the massive decade-in-the-making list of changes between XP and 7. (In Microsoft's defense, they didn't purposefully create all these huge changes at once; it's just that we all chose to ignore the intermediary stepping-stone called Vista. So for most of us, these are massive XP-to-7 changes.)

You probably know that there are many books written on how to migrate to Windows 7 from Windows XP, but a 30-second overview of the challenges is that we have to deal with new application compatibility, new hardware, x64 instead of 32-bit, a new version of Windows user profiles, a new security model, and the fact that there's no direct XP-to-7 upgrade path. The bottom line is that getting from Windows XP to Windows 7 is a lot of work and a *major* project, all set against the countdown clock ticking toward April 8, 2014—the day Microsoft ends extended support for XP.

Keep in mind that having to do a major desktop platform migration is nothing new. Windows NT 3.51 to 4.0 was also huge, as was Windows 95 to Windows 2000. But, unfortunately, the people who did those migrations have moved on. (They're probably the VMware server experts in your company now!) So for many of the people currently in charge of your Windows XP-to-Windows 7 migration, this is the first time they've faced the daunting task of redesigning the desktop from the ground up.

Since it's their first time, they're vulnerable. Your current desktop architects are susceptible to the "there's a better way" marketing blitz. It means they listen when people tell them that desktop virtualization can fix their pain.

Seasoned desktop experts know that moving from Windows XP to Windows 7 is no different than any other major desktop migration of the past fifteen years. The desktop life cycle—from the provisioning to the deployment to the patching to the maintaining to the planning—is the same today as it was in 1997. (We had SMS back then. We had Ghost. We had the policies and lockdown.)

It's also unfortunate that even those of us ready for the classic migration to Windows 7 work for managers and IT executives who have been hearing this "virtualization is a better way" message for years. A lot of us work at companies where virtualization *is* a better way for our servers and data centers. So when the people who made our servers better by virtualizing our data centers tell your boss that they can do the same thing for the desktops, your boss is going to listen. The people selling desktop virtualization will cite all the points we just made to justify their view that the desktop industry is stagnant, that stagnant industries are ripe for revolution, and that the time is now!

We lowly desktop people try to point out that desktops are different than servers, and while we're happy that server virtualization was so successful, desktop virtualization is different. Unfortunately, our meek opposition is lost in a tsunami of "virtualization is awesome" and "if server virtualization was great for physical servers, then desktop virtualization must be great for physical desktops."

Why Server Virtualization Is Great

Remember the first time you heard of this virtualization thing? Industry veterans like to point out that virtualization has been around since the mainframe days, but let's get real. We're talking about Windows desktops here. In the x86 Windows-based world, VMware invented virtualization. For most of us, it came in the form of VMware Workstation, which we used on our laptops so that we could carry our test labs with us.

This was *years* before people even considered virtualizing important production things—VMware Workstation was simply a workstation-based lab tool for most people. VMware did have "server" versions of their products, but most people didn't consider them legitimate enough for important things. Of course that changed over time, and by the mid-2000s, companies were starting to consider moving certain production servers onto the new virtual platforms.

The main selling point of server virtualization in those days was that it could enable companies to save money through server consolidation. Rather than paying for entire servers that might run at only 20% utilization, a company could run five or six of them as VMs on the same physical server. They'd save costs on hardware and data center space, and have lower power and cooling bills.

Over time, the VMware server virtualization products got better and better, and as they did, people converted more and more of their physical servers to virtual ones. And the benefits just kept on piling up. In addition to being cheaper, companies realized that they could actually have higher levels of availability with virtual servers, since they could "migrate" a running virtual server from one physical host server to another. It was also easier for companies to build new servers, since they could run any virtual server on any physical piece of hardware—they didn't have to worry about specific drivers or special software, and each new IT project didn't require the purchase of additional physical servers.

In the meantime, server hardware was getting faster and more powerful. Intel had recently changed tactics and started building more cores into each processor instead of simply making processors faster. This meant that most traditional software applications—which were not written to make use of all these cores—couldn't take advantage of them. So companies learned that even if they wanted to run a piece of software on the "bare metal" physical server, they would hit performance limits. But if instead they ran multiple instances of that software as virtual servers on a single VMware host, there was no limit to the performance they could get!

It wasn't too long before virtualization crossed the tipping point, where companies weren't asking themselves *if* they could use virtualization, but rather whether any servers should *not* be virtualized. The entire x86 server industry moved from 100% physical servers to almost 100% virtual servers in under five years!

Meanwhile in Florida...

VMware's success with virtualization at this time was based on the virtualization of servers. While this was happening, a separate group of IT professionals were doing something called server-based computing (SBC). The idea with SBC is that instead of a Windows desktop application running locally on the desktop computer the user is sitting at, the Windows application runs on a server in a central location. The user just sees a remote picture of what the program is doing. It's like having the monitor, keyboard, and mouse connected to the main computer by wires that are miles long.

While it sounds like needless complexity, there are plenty of scenarios where this SBC makes sense. For example, if a company has computers in dangerous, theft-prone, or dirty locations, SBC means that the Windows desktop applications can run in a central, safe, and clean room while the users are in the dirty environment. If a user's computer breaks or is stolen, replacing it is fast and easy, since all the software programs and configuration are safe and sound in the central location.

This type of technology is also great for scenarios where software programs are updated frequently. Imagine if you had 100 users who all needed to use a software program that changes often. Under the old way of doing things, you'd have to walk around to every single desktop or laptop computer and update the software. (And if your users are not in the same city as you, good luck with that!) But with the SBC model, you can simply update your software on the one centralized server, and *voila!*—the next time users connect, they're connecting right into the single centralized (and now updated) software.

This concept of SBC was pioneered by Fort Lauderdale-based software company Citrix Systems in the 1990s with a product called Citrix WinFrame. Microsoft caught wind of what Citrix was doing, and the two companies worked together to bring this SBC technology into the mainstream, creating a special Terminal Server edition of Windows NT 4.0. After that, Microsoft built the Terminal Server technologies into the Windows Server product itself, and while its name changed from Terminal Server to Remote Desktop Session Host (RDSH), you can still find this joint Citrix-Microsoft technology in Windows Server 2008 R2 and Windows 8 Server.

Even as Microsoft sold Windows Server with SBC capabilities built in, Citrix continued to make add-on enhancement products for the SBC market. Citrix WinFrame evolved to become MetaFrame, then Presentation Server, and finally today's Citrix XenApp. Other third-party companies joined the fray, too, with Quest Software, Ericom Software, 2X, and others leveraging the SBC capability that's built into every copy of Windows Server.

All of these SBC products were (and still are) very popular. Today, there are somewhere between 75 and 100 million licenses in circulation for these various products, and sales of the Citrix XenApp SBC product are over a billion dollars a year.

Moving from Servers Back to Desktops

Let's jump back to our conversation about VMware and server virtualization. In the late 2000s, when Citrix and Microsoft were having great success with SBC, VMware was enjoying great success with their server virtualization products. Server virtualization was one of the rare technologies whose benefits were almost universal. By this time, VMware was a public company and a major force in the IT industry. Server virtualization was ubiquitous, and even Microsoft found themselves trying to play "catch up" and entering the server virtualization game.

VMware was happy. But people wondered what would happen to VMware long term? Sure, VMware caught Microsoft off guard and was the undisputed leader of the server virtualization space. But Microsoft would surely catch up after five or ten years, and then what would happen to VMware? Would they go down as another one-trick company that was ultimately driven to bankruptcy by Microsoft?

Around this time, it started to occur to the VMware executives, partners, and investors that merely focusing on the servers in the data center was really limiting VMware's potential. If there were 50 million servers in the world that could be virtualized, then surely there must be 500 million desktops! And just think about the great benefits of virtualization: cost savings, higher availability, security, and manageability—who wouldn't want that for their desktops, too?

And so the great race to virtualize desktops began. VMware had a mission: convert as many desktops as possible to virtual machines. Run them on fancy, expensive, and (most importantly) VMware-based servers. Let the world enjoy the benefits of their newly virtualized desktops, and let VMware shareholders enjoy the cash from all those VMware server licenses they would sell.

VMware and Citrix: Frenemies from the Start?

Remember that the Citrix SBC technology involved moving Windows desktop applications off of users' desktops and into the data center. That meant that companies ended up having racks and racks of "Citrix servers." And remember that VMware's success was in converting physical servers into virtual servers. So when virtualization crossed the tipping point in the data center, a lot of Citrix servers were swept up into it as customers clamored to virtualize as many servers as they could.

Back in those days, Citrix and VMware were friends. They released joint reference architectures explaining how to run Citrix servers on VMware virtualization hosts. It was a win-win situation, since VMware got to sell more server virtualization licenses and Citrix got to leverage the virtualization technology that let customers squeeze better performance from their hardware.

But that all changed one day when VMware decided to challenge Citrix head on.

VMware's core business was built around converting physical computers into virtual computers. So while VMware had tens of millions of servers converted, there were hundreds of millions of desktops that were still running as physical computers. If VMware could convert those desktops into virtual machines, that could be worth billions of dollars per year in additional VMware licenses. But desktops don't live in the data center—they live on users' desks. So how could they all be converted to VMware virtual machines?

Simple. VMware had to first convince customers that it made sense to move their desktop computers from the users' desks and homes into the data center. From there, it would be an easy step to get everyone to run these data center-based desktops on VMware-based servers.

But how could VMware convince people to move their desktops from their desks into the data center? For this, they borrowed a play from Citrix. Citrix, after all, had been touting the benefits of SBC for years. (And remember, SBC means users run Windows desktop applications in the data center that users remotely connect to). VMware jumped on the fact that Citrix's SBC software—while considered to be very successful—was actually only used by about 50 million people. Considering there were 500-to-700 million corporate desktops in the world, VMware tried to position their own VDI solution as being appropriate for the "other 90%" of the world's users who could benefit from the advantages of having their desktops in the data center but who couldn't due to the limitations of Citrix's SBC. In other words, VMware positioned VDI as having the benefits of SBC without the downsides.

That said, the *advantages* of running Windows desktop applications in the data center and connecting remotely were the same regardless of whether a user was using the Citrix SBC or VMware VDI.

Fortunately for VMware, there was one key difference between what they wanted to do and what Citrix was doing. Citrix's SBC solution was based on users installing a special version of Microsoft Windows Server. (Remember that thing called Terminal Server that's now called RDSH?) This special version of Windows allowed multiple users to all log into the same Windows Server copy at the same time in the data center. While that was very efficient—it could support hundreds of desktop users on a single server—it was also quirky. Terminal Server didn't work with all software programs. VMware decided to jump on the "quirkiness" challenge of SBC to show that their own VDI solution could provide the desktops in the data center without the quirkiness of what Citrix was doing. So VMware went out into the world and said, "Hey, you've been using that Citrix SBC software for ten years. It's fine, but it only works for maybe 10% of your users or 10% of your applications. Well, we have a better way that can work for many more of your users."

And you know what? CIOs listened to them! After all, VMware was the company that revolutionized the servers in the data center. They delivered on all of their promises to lower costs while increasing flexibility. Everyone loved them, and any rank-and-file VMware sales rep was able to get a meeting with any CIO. So meet they did! VMware told the world that they were now going to do for desktops what they had already done for servers. And just like that, VDI was one of the top items on everyone's to-do list!

VDI: VMware's Original Desktop Virtualization Strategy

When VMware hit the ground with their desktop virtualization story, they set out to explain it as VDI, or virtual desktop infrastructure. The idea is that instead of each user having his or her own Windows computer on a desk, the users would instead have a virtual computer running on a VMware server sitting in a data center somewhere. Then the users would connect remotely from simple terminal-like devices called thin clients or existing PCs.

On the surface, VMware's VDI solution looked a lot like Citrix's existing SBC solution. And, in fact, they were very similar except for one core difference: The VMware VDI solution allowed each user to connect to his or her own "normal" desktop operating system. (In other words, it was just the regular copy of Windows XP, except that it was running remotely in a data center.) VMware called this a benefit because it was the regular desktop OS with full application support and nothing new to learn. While this was all true and certainly an advantage over Citrix's specialized server solution, there was one key difference: Because the VMware VDI solution required a separate virtual computer for each user, it required *much* more hardware in the data center to serve the same number of users. While a typical $4,000 server with the Citrix software could run well over 100 users, the same $4,000 server running the VMware VDI software could hold only 15 to 20 users.

Of course VMware did what they could to spin that, and Citrix did what they could to attack VMware.

VMware claimed (rightly so) that comparing VMware VDI to Citrix SBC was like comparing apples to oranges. Sure, VMware VDI was more expensive, but because it was running the regular desktop OS (which provided better application compatibility), it had the advantage of being able to *completely replace* a user's desktop computer. Citrix SBC, on the other hand, couldn't run certain software programs. That meant that most customers who used Citrix limited their use to certain key applications while their users still had full-blown desktop or laptop computers.

Looking back on that Citrix-VMware war of 2006, we can say there was truth to both arguments. There were scenarios where the VDI model made sense, and there where scenarios where the SBC model made sense. (And, most importantly, there were scenarios where neither made sense and a user's best choice was to continue using his or her existing desktop or laptop computer the "old way.")

The problem (or advantage, depending on your perspective) was that the old way didn't have any cheerleaders. (Well, it did, but the cheerleaders didn't have any influence.) VMware was the darling of the IT industry and virtualization was all the rage. Everyone was all hopped up on VMware and the advantages of virtualization, and no one seemed to be thinking straight. Even Citrix caught the virtualization bug, suddenly claiming one day that their own ten-year-old SBC software was actually a form of desktop virtualization, and that they themselves had been doing desktop virtualization longer than VMware. Citrix would even go on to spend $500 million to buy virtualization software company XenSource and ultimately release the Citrix XenServer virtualization product to compete directly against VMware's server virtualization products. Crazy!

So that's how we got into the whole "VDI is awesome" mess that we're in today. In the next chapter, we'll look at what people thought they were going to get with the promise of VDI. After that, we'll look at what the reality of VDI turned out to be. (It wasn't all bad. In fact, there are millions of users who are happily using VDI today, so we'll look at where it worked and where it didn't.)

One final note about terminology: In today's world, we encourage people to use the term "desktop virtualization" to define the general concept of moving beyond traditional PCs. When VMware started pushing VDI in 2006, most people used the terms "VDI" and "desktop virtualization" interchangeably. We'll eventually get into the differences (in Chapter 5), but until then, we're focusing on VDI specifically, since that's what most people think of when they think of desktop virtualization and that's what VMware was pushing when they decided to attack the desktop market.

Chapter 2

The Promise of VDI

In this chapter, we're going to look at all the promises made by those who pushed VDI in the mid-2000s, including sales reps, vendors, consultants, and partners. You might think that some of these claims are far-fetched, too good to be true, or just plain B.S. You're not alone! But everything covered in this chapter was pulled directly from actual marketing materials, slides, product slicks, and articles touting the many benefits of VDI.

Keep in mind that while this chapter is called "The Promise of VDI," the next chapter is "The Reality of VDI." If you're a seasoned industry professional, skip to the next chapter.

As a quick side note, we touch on a lot of technology concepts here (app virtualization, SBC, provisioning, etc.). We'll dig deeper into all of these throughout the book, so if there's anything you don't fully understand now, you'll be caught up soon.

The 15 Promises of VDI

Again, all fifteen benefits described below have actually been promised by VDI marketers over the past six years. It was hard for us to not laugh out loud while compiling some of these, but we swear that we didn't make any of them up.

Promise No. 1: Saves money

Almost every single feature of VDI promises lower cost, mostly through a lower total cost of ownership (TCO). Thin clients are cheaper than fat clients. Licensing is cheaper with VDI. Users can be more productive when using VDI. Thin clients use less electricity and last longer. There's less downtime. It's easier to manage images when they're all in one place. Provisioning takes only a few mouse clicks instead of the hours it takes to install software. The refrain is the same with every vendor, again and again: VDI will save you money.

Promise No. 2: Better security

With VDI, no data is stored on the client endpoint at all. If somebody steals a thin client, then congratulations, they now have possession of a worthless paperweight! When virtual desktops are accessed from personal laptops, tablets, home computers, and other devices, no corporate data is at risk. Sure, your users will be sad if they lose their personal laptop, and maybe they're out the $1,000 it cost them, but that's far better than the millions of dollars your company could lose if a laptop containing sensitive data were lost.

With VDI, all of that sensitive data resides exclusively within your own data center. You're already used to securing your storage appliances, servers, and networks through tough digital and physical means—now all of your users' day-to-day data can have the exact same high-quality protection.

Extra security features can be built into client devices used to access the VDI environment as well, and users won't have to spend extra time trying to figure out how to use them. Private tunnels, SSL VPNs, and proxies can simply work automatically when they're built into soft clients, web portals, or thin clients.

Promise No. 3: Users can work from anywhere, via any device

VDI is great for "bring your own device" programs and for accommodating the consumerization of IT. When users want to bring MacBooks and iPads into the enterprise, there's no need to turn them away. Before VDI, supporting these devices would have been a nightmare ("How do I get this Mac joined to the domain so it can print?") With VDI, however, IT can get out of the endpoint management game entirely.

And when we say that VDI desktops can be accessed from any device, we mean any device at all! There are clients for Mac OS X, Windows, Linux, iOS, Android, BlackBerry, and others, and web clients ensure that devices without native clients still have access to VDI desktops. Web clients are also useful for when users connect from public computers, such as hotel kiosks or Internet cafes, or even from a friend's computer.

Users can even take their images offline. Since desktop hypervisors can often run the exact same VM disk images as servers, it's simply a matter of a user downloading their VM image before they go offline. Now users can stay productive when traveling on airplanes or when out in the field, while still having the benefits of VDI.

Promise No. 4: The user experience will be awesome

Remote display protocols are getting better all the time, so every year there are great leaps in user experience. In the late 2000s, the Web 2.0 revolution took off, making rich audio and media commonplace across the Internet. Advances in remote display protocols were right there, ready to bring that new experience to users.

As a matter of fact, remote display protocols handle so much more than just displays these days that they should really be called just "remoting protocols." Users can send audio and video up to the remote host, they can use remote touch gestures, and it's possible to use almost any USB peripheral imaginable. Over time, it's getting harder and harder for users to even tell their desktop is located in a distant data center.

Meanwhile, as the user experience is becoming richer, remote protocols are continuously improving their bandwidth footprint, taking less and less bandwidth with each new release. Organizations are able to avoid costly investments in faster networks, and can instead use existing resources more efficiently.

Promise No. 5: VDI is environmentally friendly

A typical desktop PC uses about 400 watts of power. Thin clients and zero clients can use as little as 15 watts. That's more than 25 times less power usage for each user. Multiply that by everyone in your office, and your company will be saving a lot of energy. VDI is good for the environment.

Also, since users can work from anywhere with VDI, organizations can allow more employees to work from home, reducing office space requirements. After all, offices (especially branch offices) that are used for only 40 out of 168 hours a week are inefficient anyway, so why not eliminate them?

More employees working from home (or their favorite coffee shop or park) also means fewer commuting miles driven, further easing strains on energy resources.

Promise No. 6: Client devices last longer

It's a known fact that today's hottest computer will be old news in six to eight months. Unfortunately, most companies replace their PCs on four-year cycles, leaving employees to work on out-of-date devices most of the time.

With thin clients, the same device can serve a continually evolving desktop environment for years on end. There are VDI installations that use the same client devices for a decade! Even if you don't choose to keep your thin clients that long, hardware refresh cycles will still be much more inconsequential than with desktops.

In addition, these cheap, long-lasting thin and zero clients take up very little space on users' desks. No longer is there a hulking, noisy box to get in the way and throw off heat—instead, employees can use that space to be more comfortable and productive. Also keep in mind that you don't have to throw away all those PCs that get retired when VDI programs are implemented. For more budget-minded organizations, those PCs can become the new thin clients. An old, out-of-date PC is still an excellent thin client for years to come. (And the best part is that if you leave the PCs on all your employees' desks, they won't complain about IT "taking their computer away" when they get switched over to a VDI desktop!)

Promise No. 7: Reduced downtime due to hardware failure, on the server or the client

We already mentioned that thin clients have much longer lifespans than PCs, and we can add to that that their lack of moving parts and low level of complexity means they hardly ever break. Thin clients can withstand high heat, moisture, and dust much better than traditional desktops. And when they do break, it's no big deal because they are generally much cheaper than PCs.

When it comes to personal computers, there are many different manufacturers providing dizzying arrays of options and price points. Unfortunately, this wide range also means that some PCs just aren't very high quality and might not be good enough for enterprise use. With VDI, though, since the endpoint doesn't affect performance, stability, or security, the risk of PC failure is completely moot.

Instead, your desktops are running on server hardware, which is built to much higher specifications than PC hardware. Failures are much less common, and when they do occur, redundancy features ensure that users won't even notice.

Promise No. 8: Better disaster recovery and business continuity

Having desktops in the data center means they'll be covered by all the same disaster recovery protections that servers have always had. Should the worst happen, your business can rest assured that there won't be any disruption to service.

Also, if something should happen that forces all your users to work from alternate locations, using VDI means that they can still have access to their normal everyday desktops. This is much better than traditional scenarios that have a bunch of old, slow, and different emergency PCs.

Promise No. 9: Easier image management

It seems like PCs deployed on a wide scale get more difficult to manage every day. In many office environments, even going from one workstation to another is a hassle. But when every single user's image is right there in the data center, management is much easier.

In the VDI world, when updates are pushed out to desktops, all the traffic stays in the data center, where high speed and capacity are built in. There's no need to slow down your company's entire network on patch day.

If it's necessary to rebuild a user's computer, it can be done in an instant. There's no need to take the physical hardware away from the employee's desk, erase the hard drive, reinstall Windows, reinstall applications, carry it back to the user, then have the user reconfigure all their personal settings. Instead, the user might not even know that they are getting a new image!

Promise No. 10: Simpler provisioning

Whether to bring on a new user or simply refresh an existing one, new desktop virtual machines can be created in a matter of seconds using VDI. There's no more waiting around for hours, clicking Next, Next, Next while Windows installs on a client device. With VDI, you only have to install Windows and each program once—ever!

Other techniques associated with VDI, such as layering, mean that a disk image can be assembled dynamically. You can use a base image containing core operating system components for all images, companywide. Then you can create an application layer to go on top of that to create what looks like different images for different departments. Once again, this is all done by copying existing images—there's no need to ever build something from the ground up.

Promise No. 11: Better user isolation

One of the biggest challenges of Terminal Server-based forms of SBC is that multiple users all log into the same copy of Windows, so they share one disk image, operating environment, and set of resources. This poses a few challenges.

First, because you have a bunch of users all sharing the same copy of Windows, all your users get the exact same experience and same applications. If all the users need the same stuff, this is fine. But if you have a diverse group of users that all need different sets of apps, it's really hard to put them all on the same Terminal Server.

Second, Windows desktop applications were never designed to be used by multiple users at the same time. Some of them flat out don't work in the shared Terminal Server environment.

Finally, users are the wild card when it comes to performance. Having a lot of users all logged into Windows at the same time might be fine until one of them decides to repaginate a 200-page document in Word, causing everyone else to sit and wait with an hourglass cursor while the first user's document is processed.

VDI, on the other hand, allows each user to have his or her own isolated virtual machine. Each user can have a different set of software, since each VM runs a different copy of Windows. All the "normal" Windows software works, since VDI is just running a normal single-user copy of the Windows desktop OS. And if one user goes crazy in his session, the hypervisor can clamp down on it to ensure that the performance of the other VMs is not compromised.

Promise No. 12: More consistent performance

With VDI, there's no need to worry about whether a user is using a run-of-the-mill laptop, a powerful desktop, or even a convenient—but possibly underpowered—netbook, because all the endpoint has to be able to do is run a simple desktop client.

On the data center side, the consistent performance is ensured by the features of virtualization. VMs can be moved from one physical hardware host to another. If a power user starts taking up too much memory, new users that come on can be routed to different host servers or that power user can be live-migrated to a different server.

Application virtualization used on top of VDI works even better than application virtualization on top of traditional desktops. Since the applications and the desktops can be in the same data center, there's no need to stream an entire application across the WAN. Instead, it's a quick hop on the LAN.

Promise No. 13: Licensing is easier

Now that organizations don't have to worry about getting special multi-user versions of software, organizations can simply purchase volume quantities of conventional Windows desktop software.

Being able to keep track of what all the users are doing means that it's easier to keep track of pooled licenses. Organizations can save money by reducing the number of extra licenses needed for concurrent-user licensed products.

Also, licenses for VDI products themselves are often bundled together with licenses for other virtualization and SBC technologies. It's easy to move over to VDI when the licenses are already there.

Promise No. 14: You already have the servers and technology

Server virtualization has been a windfall for countless organizations. Since server virtualization freed up space in your data center anyway, you might as well use it for desktops! Now that server space is a commodity, there's no need to worry about what goes in there. You just have space, and it works. That same space or server capacity can be used to host desktops just as easily as it can be used to host servers.

This also breaks down the divide between server admins and desktop admins—since everything is on the same platform now, administrators can be more flexible and collaborate more easily.

Promise No. 15: You already know how to do virtualization

The fifteenth and final promise of VDI is that since it's running desktop VMs on the same platform that runs your server VMs, you already have the skills to do everything! Your engineers already know how to set up VMware servers, they're all certified, and they're ready to go. The hard part is done!

Sounds Amazing!

And there you have it. VDI sounds pretty great, doesn't it? Remember, every one of these fifteen promises comes from actual marketing materials pushing VDI. So what do you think? Is it all true? In the next chapter, we're going to look at the reality of VDI and which of these promises are real and which have turned out to be complete myths.

Chapter 3

The Reality of VDI

HAVE YOU EVER THOUGHT THAT IF VDI WERE SO GOOD, why are we all arguing about whether 2012 or 2013 will be the "year of VDI?" If it were that awesome, wouldn't it just be the way we did things now?

It's hard to know precisely how many people in the world actually use VDI because vendors only count the number of licenses they've sold, not actual deployments. (And a lot of those "sold" licenses were actually given away or bundled with other products.) Add to that the fact that some vendors (Citrix) bundle VDI with other non-VDI products, so even if a customer buys and implements one of these products, we still don't know if they're actually using VDI.

The only thing we do know is that the total percentage of VDI users in the world (as compared with traditional desktop users) is small. Estimates vary depending on whom you ask, but most people agree that we're looking at single-digit percentages. If you consider that there are somewhere between 500 million and 700 million corporate desktops in the world (again, the exact number depends on how you count), we're probably looking at only five-to-ten million using VDI. (In other words, maybe 2%?)

So the reality of VDI is that it's not in widespread use. This is a sharp contrast to server virtualization, which is huge. Why is that?

The obvious answer is that VDI just flat out doesn't live up to the hype. It doesn't matter if you like VDI or hate it—mathematically speaking, something with only 2% market penetration just isn't a major game changer. If VDI were so great, we'd see the usage explode just like we did with server virtualization.

So what gives? Why isn't everyone using it? We believe there are three main reasons:

- A VDI desktop is not inherently easier to manage than a traditional, non-VDI desktop. So the automatic "management benefit" is a myth.

- VDI desktops run in the data center. Users run out in the world. Putting a network between users and their desktops creates challenges, including performance issues, peripheral complexities, and the fact that users can't work if there's no Internet connection.

- Even though VDI is sold as having lower TCO or being cheaper than traditional desktops, the reality is that when comparing apples to apples, VDI is more expensive than existing desktops. So if a customer really cared about saving money, they would not choose VDI.

We understand that these are three fairly damning statements about VDI, so we're going to spend many of the next pages of this chapter discussing why we think this is true. But remember, this chapter is about the reality of VDI, and the reality is that there are plenty of scenarios where VDI is awesome and people love it. (After all, five-to-ten million users is nothing to sneeze at!) So we'll end this chapter by exploring where VDI is working and when it makes sense.

But first, we'll begin with our exploration of the challenges and myths of VDI.

Myth No. 1: VDI Is Easier to Manage than Traditional PCs

One of the first things we hear from people wanting to sell VDI is that VDI desktops are easier to manage than traditional PC desktops. The primary "evidence" cited is the fact that VDI allows multiple users to share a single disk image. They'll pitch it something like this:

With traditional PCs, each PC has its own hard drive running its own applications and its own copy of Windows. So if you have 100 users, that means there are 100 disks you need to maintain, patch, update, fix, install, and deal with. But if you switch to VDI, all of your users can share a single master disk image, meaning you only have to manage a single copy of Windows for all 100 users. Obviously, that's much easier to manage!

On the surface, this seems true. (Too good to be true, perhaps?) But when you dig deeper, you learn there's a reason that all your users have their own copy of Windows. It's because all your users are different! They all run different applications and they each do different things. The reality is that it's difficult, if not impossible, to take an environment where you have 100 users with 100 individual computers with 100 different sets of software, data, and configurations and to consolidate that down to a single master image.

Think about it: If all your users share the same disk image, that means they all share the same software and they all share the same configuration. How in the world do you suppose that you can just magically get all your users, who are used to doing whatever they want, to suddenly give up their own personalities and just start using a generic shared image?

But isn't a single image simpler to manage?

The irony of this is that managing a single image is cheaper and easier than managing hundreds of separate images. But the people pushing VDI try to pull a fast one here when they claim that this is an advantage of VDI, because if you really wanted to, you could just use a single master image for all your traditional PCs and get the management savings without VDI at all.

Again, say you have 100 traditional PC users. You could build a locked-down, perfect "gold" image for all of those PCs. Since that image is locked down, it would be simple to manage because the users wouldn't be able to install anything of their own. (And if users can't install anything of their own, you can just re-image the machines willy-nilly whenever you need to update them.) This would be *much* cheaper than a world where users are able do whatever they want.

But remember the kicker: *you don't need VDI to get that!* You can just lock down your existing machines.

So what we have here is a classic trick where the VDI people are trying to say that it's the VDI that's making things easier to manage, when in fact it's not that at all—the management savings are coming from you locking down all your computers in order for them to share that master image.

What about VDI without that single image?

In the previous chapter, we looked at all the wonderful things that VDI promised, and many (if not all) of those advantages were less about VDI and more about the fact that users' desktops would be moved off of their desks and into the data center.

Now imagine that you have your existing pre-VDI environment with your 100 users, each with their own desktop. Everything is humming along just fine. Then one day you read about this great thing called VDI and you think you want it because putting users' desktops in the data center would give them the flexibility to work from any device and the security of everything centralized. That sounds great!

So you decide you just want to convert all your desktops to VDI to get that. But then the people selling you the VDI tell you that in order to go to VDI, you also have to convert all of your users so that they're sharing a single master disk image!! That's where things get crazy. Here all you wanted was to move your desktops into the data center, and the VDI people are telling you that you have to fundamentally change the way your desktops work by locking everything down and going with a shared image. So what gives? Why is that the case?

The reality is that hardware in the data center is much more expensive than desktop and laptop hardware. In your existing pre-VDI world, each user has his or her own PC with its own hard drive. Each user's hard drive has its own copy of Windows installed, plus the user's apps, data, and settings. The users are each able to do whatever they want, since they're each running their own computer, so what they do doesn't affect other users.

But when it comes to VDI, you have possibly 100 users all sharing the same computer in the data center. This means that if one user does something that requires a lot of resources, the other users are negatively affected. (Or it means the system steps in to prevent that user from affecting everyone else, but that just negatively affects the first user.)

The biggest bottleneck, when compared with traditional PCs, is the hard disks. First, imagine if each of your users has 40GB of hard drive space consumed on their existing desktop computers. If you move all those users to VDI, that means you'll need 4TB of primary bootable storage space in your data center for those same 100 users. (And remember, primary storage in data centers is really expensive.) You'll also need to ensure that your storage is fast enough for your users. Most servers today have, what, maybe eight hard drives in them? No matter what type of RAID configuration you do, those eight drives are not going to be fast enough to serve 100-plus users, each with their own 40GB hard drive image.

This is where the notion of all your users sharing a single disk image comes into play. Not only does sharing mean that all your users take up less space, but since only a single "master" image is shared by many users, it's really easy to cache the contents of that image in SSD or memory, giving essentially unlimited performance. (And frankly, when you do this, your disk is no longer a performance bottleneck for your VDI server.)

So you think, "Great! Problem solved! I'll just do this single master image sharing thing and VDI will be awesome!" But remember how we started this section? If the users in your pre-VDI environment each had their own disks with their own applications, how exactly are you going to magically migrate from a world where everyone is different to the world of VDI where everyone has to be the same?

No, really? How are you going to do that? Because we'd like to know! Seriously, if it were that easy, you would have moved to a locked-down image for your traditional desktops ten years ago and started saving those management costs way back then. Even if you "image" your traditional desktops today, that base image is still heavily modified once users start using it.

This goes back to the original point that it would be cool to use VDI for your users but not have to change the way you manage them. In other words, if you could let all your users have their own unique, persistent disk image and still use VDI. While that is possible today, it's very expensive. Doing so requires some kind of third-party additional storage or speedy storage controller. And if you justified moving to VDI to save money, building the storage infrastructure to support the needed performance for hundreds of users to each have their own disk image would blow your cost model out of the water!

What about app virtualization and user personalization?

When explaining this VDI management savings myth, inevitably someone will interrupt us claiming that we're wrong. They'll say that users can share the same non-persistent master image as the base image only, and then you simply use tools like app virtualization and user environment virtualization to deliver a layer of customization and personalization on top of it. So it's the best of both worlds! (High performance and the low cost of a shared master image with the personalization capabilities of individual personal images.) Again, we have to call B.S. on this:

Let's start with app virtualization. The term "app virtualization" can apply to a few different types of technologies, but the gist is that the apps are delivered into a Windows environment in a way that does not involve installing them onto the computer in the traditional manner.

One type of app virtualization allows the apps to be "streamed" into the Windows environment, where they run in their own isolated bubble, guaranteeing they won't interfere with other apps (and relieving the administrator of tedious compatibility and regression testing). Products that work this way include Microsoft App-V, VMware ThinApp, InstallFree, Symantec Workspace Virtualization, Endeavors, and Spoon.net.

Another type of app virtualization involves running Windows desktop applications on remote computers and then having the user connect to just the single app from their desktop. This is based on the SBC technology we discussed in Chapter 1. Products that offer this include Microsoft Windows' RemoteApp feature, Citrix XenApp, Quest Software's vWorkspace, and Ericom PowerTerm WebConnect.

Both of these types of technologies do a great job delivering a personalized set of applications to a user, even if that user logs onto a generic, shared "master" desktop. (So it might be a generic desktop before the user logs on, but once they're in, app virtualization will give them all their own apps.) So you might think, "This is perfect! Now my shared master image VDI dream has come true!"

Except for one thing: Not all of the world's applications are compatible with these various app virtualization products! In fact, there are plenty of apps that simply *cannot be virtualized*, period! (The exact percentage of apps that can be virtualized varies based on which product you're using and how skilled the IT folks who are doing the virtualization are.) But the truth is that no single product can virtualize 100% of your applications. And whether you can virtualize 90%, 95%, or 99.9% is irrelevant—it only takes one single "non-virtualizable" app for your whole model to break down. If you come across an app that you can't virtualize but you're basing your whole VDI plan on the fact that you're going to share a single master image and deliver apps based on what users actually need, what do you do now? Do you tell that user that he or she can't use the app in question? Do you just not use VDI for certain users? Or do you build a VDI environment that's orders of magnitude more expensive so that you can give each user their own "real" desktop instead of relying on the disk image sharing scheme?

Seriously? What do you do? Because none of these answers is good! (We'll explore app virtualization more toward the end of the book, when we look at how you can build a desktop and app delivery strategy for the future.)

Moving beyond the app issues, we could have the exact same conversation about the various "user personalization" products. Much like the app virtualization products that deliver a customized set of applications to a user after he or she logs onto a shared master disk image, user personalization products maintain all of a user's personalization settings. (Think backgrounds, Outlook settings, custom dictionaries, app configuration settings, etc.) There are plenty of vendors offering products in this space, including AppSense, RES Software, Scense, and triCerat. The Big Three desktop virtualization vendors (Citrix, VMware, and Quest Software) also have these user personalization capabilities.

But again, there are bound to be settings that these products can't quite handle. So when you find that some of your users can't get their environment built back perfectly on top of the shared master disk image, what do you do? Do you just pull those users out of your VDI environment? Is that even an option?

What about persistent shared disk images?

At this point, the people selling VDI usually interrupt, saying something along the lines of, "Not true! We can 'persist' the user part of the shared disk image, so when users log in again, they can have their changes back."

But this is also hogwash. To understand why, we have to dig under the covers a bit to examine how this whole disk image sharing thing works in the first place.

Let's take a look at what a VDI host server might look like. In the drawing below, a single VDI server is hosting eight virtual desktops. (In real life, it would host a lot more than eight, but eight is simpler to show.) If these eight virtual desktops were like physical desktops, they would each have their own disk drive (which is a VMDK or VHD file for virtual desktops).

This is a VDI environment with no image sharing. It's a "personal" or "persistent" disk mode, which is nice because each user can have completely different software. The downside is that you have to manage these desktops the "old" way, with software patching and such.

We already mentioned that people who love VDI claim that a better solution is for all the VDI users to share a single disk image. That way you only have to update one disk image to instantly update lots of virtual desktops. Let's draw what that might look like with our eight virtual desktops:

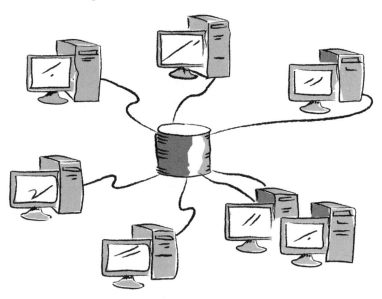

The technical problem is that it's not possible for two machines to literally share a single disk drive (even if they're virtual machines). As you can imagine, the disk drive in a computer is locked by the computer that's using it. And that computer has to write a lot of exclusive stuff to the drive, like log files, temp files, the page file, etc. So when we talk about multiple virtual desktops sharing the same disk, what they're really sharing is a single "master" disk. In fact, that master disk is locked to be read-only so that none of the individual virtual machines can write to it. Instead, each virtual machine takes whatever it wants to write to the disk and puts it off to the side in another location, like this:

Notice that the virtual desktop here is using the master disk image for its reads, and then it puts its writes into the other location. (And then of course if it needs to read something that it previously wrote, it gets it from the alternate location instead of from the master.)

So in effect, the individual virtual machine's disk "image" is actually a combination of two sources: the shared, read-only master location, plus the small sliver of changes that the desktop made previously. (We usually call the small little changes the user's delta differential file, since it includes the delta changes from the master.)

In the previous diagram, we used just one single VDI desktop as an example, but you can imagine that the same thing is happening for all the virtual desktops on that server at the same time:

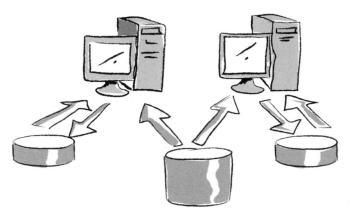

Each VDI desktop's disk is a combination of the shared master disk plus a VM-specific delta differential file. And of course this is the case for every virtual desktop on the server:

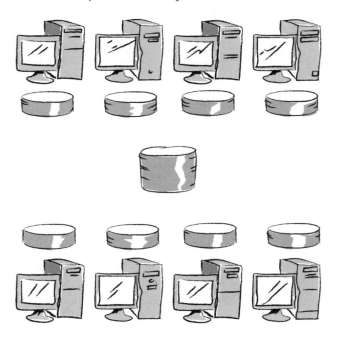

This is great for a few reasons. First, having one shared master plus only the little slivers for each VDI desktop is great for capacity, as it consumes far less space than if each desktop had its own complete image:

Of course one potential problem with this is that the shared master image is being used by lots of virtual desktops. So you can imagine that it would be easy for it to overheat and run into performance problems:

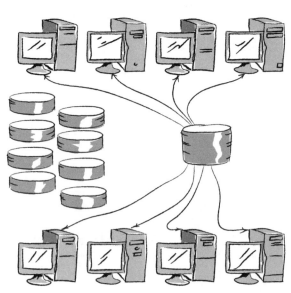

The good news, though, is that the shared master is read-only. And reads are relatively easy to cache. You can cache them in memory, put that disk image on SSD, or use any one of many other options to make it fast.

Okay, so far so good. So what's the problem? Let's take another look at an individual virtual desktop:

When the virtual desktop is new, the individual delta differential disk image file is truly a sliver, because each desktop is virtually identical to the master image. So there aren't too many changes to store in the individual delta file.

But imagine how this will change over time. Remember that everything that's written with the virtual desktop goes into that delta file. So over time, you'll get hot fixes, temp files, application updates, etc. And that means that the sliver grows and grows:

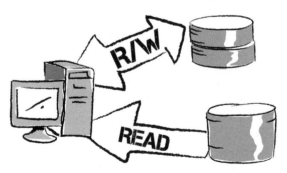

So with bigger slivers per disk, let's look at our big picture:

Hmm…It doesn't look as good as it did initially, does it? Then think about it after some more time passes. Imagine you install something huge into your VMs, like a Windows service pack or a new version of Office. Now your situation is going to look something like this:

Yikes! What happened to the capacity savings we were getting from that shared master image?

And as if that's not bad enough, we have another major problem here. Remember the trick we used to get good performance from the disk images? We were counting on the fact that all the virtual desktops were sharing the same master image file and we were therefore able to cache it or put it on an SSD.

But with the individual desktop differential disk files growing so huge, we run into a situation where most of the reads that the desktops need don't come from that super-fast shared master. Instead, each desktop is reading most of its data from its own differential file. So, yeah, all the desktops could share most of their files when the master contained the latest info. But all those new Windows files in that latest service pack? Each desktop is reading it out of its own differential file. So instead of 100 desktops on a server sharing the same cached files, you have 100 desktops each reading 100 separate files from their own delta differential disk files.

Now you're getting hurt twice! First is that the capacity you were saving by sharing that single image has evaporated, and second is that you're going to need a lot of storage bandwidth, since the individual virtual desktops are not really using the master disk image that you've planned for.

At this point, the people who are selling this idea will say, "But wait! You can fix this problem easily. All you have to do is re-compose your desktops." The idea with recomposing (each vendor has a different term for it) is that you create an updated master image with all the latest common updates that had been going into all the individual differential disk files. Then you delete each of the old bloated differential files and you're back to square one, with a fresh, up-to-date master image that has most of the info that each desktop needs and small delta differential files.

Sounds great, right? There's one major problem with this. When you re-create your master image file, you have to *destroy the delta files to start over!* So, yeah, a lot of the stuff in the old differential files was service packs and app updates that are now in the new master image, but the delta files also contained whatever else it was that the user changed since day one. (So we're talking about apps they installed, data files, preferences, plug-ins, etc.) If you blow away those delta differential files, that's essentially the same as re-imaging each user's desktop. Will your users like that?

But wait, can't we put the user data somewhere else?

Now, again, the people who love VDI are going to say that blowing away the user's desktop every time you need to update the master image is okay. They're going to say that you can create a second disk image that is a personal image for user data that is separate from the system disk. So you end up with the C: drive for the Windows and system stuff and a D: drive for all the user-specific stuff. And of course you can use policies to make this transparent to the user (so they don't even know that their desktop and things like that are going to a different location):

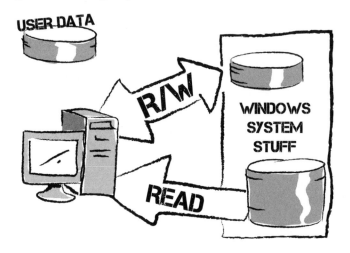

The general concept of a separate personal disk for each user is fine. The problem is that there's a lot of stuff that doesn't fit nicely into that user data disk. For example, what about applications? If the user installs an application, it's going to go into the C: drive and will be blown away when the admin rebuilds the master file.

The bottom line is the idea that you can just use a shared image as a starting point and then let your users persist their images doesn't fix anything! If you let the images live forever, you have the same performance problems you have with giving each user their own one-to-one image. And if you ever want to refresh your master disk image, you blow away the user changes, which means you have the same issues around customization and personalization that we covered at the beginning of the chapter, with the solution where all the users share a single master image. So either way, persisting these differential disk image files doesn't buy you anything.

To add insult to injury, why not just use RDSH?

Let's say you do decide that you still want to use VDI and that you want to go with the shared model, where all your users are sharing the same master disk image. As we outlined before, if you want your users to be different at all, you'll need to use app virtualization, user personal data disks, and some kind of user personalization software. Sure, we mentioned that these all have drawbacks—some apps can't be virtualized and your users can't install their own applications. But maybe that's okay for you. Maybe your environment only needs a few apps that can all be virtualized, and maybe your users don't have admin rights. In that case, isn't your environment simple enough for VDI with a shared master image?

Again, we would caution you. If your environment is simple enough that this gold master image will work, then you have to ask yourself why you're not just using Remote Desktop Session Host? (Also known as RDSH and formerly known as Terminal Server or SBC.)

In terms of server hardware, because RDSH has lots of users sharing a single instance of Windows, you only have to spend about one-fourth of the cost to build an RDSH environment versus a VDI environment with a shared master image.

And think about the main criticisms that people levy at RDSH: Users can't be admins, users can't install software, and not all applications work. Well, guess what? With your shared-disk VDI environment, users can't be admins or install software (because anything they do will be lost), and not all applications work (since you have to use app virtualization for any apps that aren't built into the gold master and used by everyone). So really the only difference between RDSH and shared VDI is that the VDI option is about four times as expensive!

To be fair, there's a lot more to the whole RDSH versus VDI conversation, and we'll dig in deeper later. But in the context of disk image sharing and management savings, shared VDI is basically the same as RDSH, except it's more expensive.

Let's go back to the "personal" VDI option

So if shared VDI doesn't make sense (since if it works for you, then you might as well use RDSH and save the money), does that mean that all VDI is worthless? Of course not! Let's go back to the concept from the beginning of the chapter, which is that sometimes it might be cool to get the benefits of VDI desktops in the data center but you don't want to change the way your users work. You don't want to change anything, really, except to move the desktop image into the data center.

If this is you, then you want personal VDI (or persistent VDI or 1-to-1 VDI)—basically VDI where each virtual desktop has its own completely separate disk image. Users can do whatever they want. They can be admins. They can install whatever they want.

Remember some people will say that this 1-to-1 VDI is impossible to manage, but we argue that if you can manage all your desktops today, you can do the same thing once they're moved into the data center to become VDI. The main problem with 1-to-1 VDI, as we touched on at the beginning of this chapter, is around the performance and storage space needed for all the individual full disk images.

And this is one of the main reasons VDI has such a low adoption rate after all these years: The only way that VDI has been technically feasible for a decent price was when all your users shared a master image, but that brought the other problems we discussed. And if you wanted to avoid those problems by giving each user their own 1-to-1 disk image, then the storage requirement was much too high and you destroyed your cost structure.

So it was lose-lose, which is why most people either stayed on RDSH or their existing physical desktops and laptops.

A quick note on the future of VDI: There are many different storage technologies just now emerging—mostly from start-up companies—that will "solve" the performance and storage problems of 1-to-1 disk images. These products can break down the underlying common storage blocks from multiple different disk images and consolidate them for performance and storage capacity improvements. This means that 1-to-1 VDI can be economically feasible from a storage standpoint, which really changes the game.

We'll look more at these later in the book, when we talk about the future of Windows. For now, we have to get back to the main point of this section, which is outlining the various challenges that have prevented VDI from living up to the hype of recent years.

Myth No. 2: Data Center Desktops Are Better Than Local Desktops

One of the realities of VDI that applies regardless of whether you're using a shared or 1-to-1 disk image is the fact that with VDI, your users' desktops are "remote." (That could be in your data center, a hosting provider's data center, or in the cloud. In each case, the desktops are running in one place while your users are in another.)

As we discussed in the first chapter, this model is conceptually no different than the RDSH SBC technology that a lot of companies have been using since the 1990s. We collectively refer to these as "desktops in the data center" technologies, since the challenges of remote Windows desktop computing are the same regardless of whether the user is connecting to VDI or RDSH.

Again, there are specific scenarios where VDI makes more sense than RDSH and vice versa. But that's not the point of this section. Right now, we're looking at the general challenges of putting a desktop in a data center, and those apply to both VDI and RDSH.

By the way, when we say "data center," we're using the term generically. Really we're talking about the desktops running on a server somewhere with the users somewhere else. But that "somewhere" where the desktops run could be a server in a closet, your own data center, a colocated or hosted data center, or even a cloud service with apps running who knows where.

So, getting back to those data center-hosted challenges, what are they?

Challenge No. 1: No offline

Perhaps this is pretty obvious, but if you put your users' desktops in the data center, users can't work if they don't have an Internet connection. It seems like every year we hear people talk about the ubiquity of wireless Internet access, and certainly 3G phones and portable hot spots have helped quite a bit. But there are still plenty of times when users are on a subway or an airplane or in another environment with a spotty connection. Do you really want to risk that your users can't work if they can't get a strong connection? (Heck, forget your users. Would you yourself want to be in a situation where your ability to do any work is tied to whether or not you have a solid Internet connection?)

Another related challenge is the fact that getting connected to a remote desktop takes more time than just opening a laptop. Imagine getting off a plane and wanting to check something real quick. With a traditional laptop, you open the lid, it wakes up, you type in your password, and boom! You're in. About three seconds total.

But with VDI, you have to open your device and unlock it. Then you have to launch your virtual desktop client connection software. (And maybe you have to wait for a MiFi to boot, or maybe you also have to connect to a VPN first.) Then you have to log into your desktop client and wait for it to find a desktop for you and establish a connection. Then you have to get logged into that desktop. What's the best case? Thirty seconds? More like 60 seconds realistically? And you have to do this every time? Yikes!

Challenge No. 2: Graphical app limitations

Those of you who've been working with Terminal Server or Citrix for a long time know that the remoting protocols that are used to connect to remote desktops have always had performance limitations. Remember how awesome Citrix MetaFrame was the first time you accessed Word from a remote computer? Now remember how much it sucked the first time you accessed YouTube?

When a user's desktop is in a data center, the mere fact that the applications are running in one location with the user interface remoted to another location presents logistical performance problems. Of course the remoting protocols (VMware PC-over-IP, Citrix HDX/ICA, Microsoft RDP/RemoteFX, etc.) have gotten better over the years, but there's still a fundamental rule that applies to all remoting protocols: good user experience, low bandwidth, and low CPU—pick any two. (This is the remoting protocol version of that old business adage "fast, cheap, and easy—pick any two.")

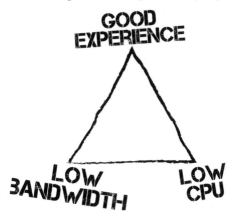

So if you want a good user experience that doesn't require a ton of bandwidth, you're going to need a lot of processing horsepower on your host and client. If you want a good user experience but you don't have a lot of processing power, then you're going to need a lot of bandwidth. And if you want low bandwidth and low CPU usage, you'd better be prepared for a bad user experience. This was true of remoting protocols in 1998, and it's still true today.

Now some people might be saying, "Hey! We have a lot more processing power now as compared to 1998, and we have a lot more bandwidth now. So that means the user experience should be great. Problem solved!"

Not so fast! While bandwidth and processing power have certainly increased since 1998, so have users' expectations of what makes a "good experience." The remoting protocols of 1998 only had to support 800x600 resolution, 256 colors, no video, no USB, and apps like Office and SAP. But today, we're trying to remote dual displays with 10x as many pixels, video, VoIP, bidirectional client audio, USB, Aero glass, 3-D, etc. So we have a sort of Moore's Law for the user experience requirements along with our CPU and bandwidth. (By the way, if you're upset that the protocol issues from 1998 haven't been solved, that's actually not true. Today's remoting protocols can deliver the crap out of a 1998 user experience!)

But in most 2012 use cases, the desktop just doesn't have the same user experience when connecting remotely versus a desktop running locally on a client device. Maybe it's bandwidth. Maybe it's server horsepower. Maybe it's client selection. Maybe it's that user expectations are too high. Regardless of the reason, the corporate world is littered with shattered ideas of how "good" the remote experience will be. And this applies to all vendors and all protocols. Remoting Windows is hard, and there are a lot of scenarios where the remote experience just doesn't cut it.

Challenge No. 3: Client peripheral complexities

Another challenge of having a desktop in the data center is the fact that any peripherals that a user wants to use are plugged into the client, but the Windows desktop is running in the data center. That means that not only does the remoting protocol (HDX, PC-over-IP, RemoteFX, etc.) have to deal with sending great graphics from the data center to the desktop, but it also has to deal with whatever random thing the user plugs in. (This is why we call them "remoting protocols" instead of "remote display protocols," since they have to deal with so much more than just the display.)

Back in the 1990s, our dream was for the remoting of USB support. And now in 2012, we have it. Heck, Windows 8 even supports USB remoting for RDSH. So that's great. Unfortunately most mainstream USB devices are USB v2 (480 Mbit/s) and we're just now starting to see USB v3 peripherals (which can be up to 5 Gbit/s). So, yeah, our remoting protocols can support USB, but if a user plugs in a USB 2 webcam that wants to reserve 200 Mbit/s on the USB bus via an isochronous connection, do you think that there's any remoting protocol or network that can deal with that? (And of course the user won't understand why it doesn't work. They just know that on their old local desktop, they could just plug in the webcam and it worked, but now with this new data center-based desktop, it doesn't. So what gives?)

Challenge No. 4: Data center real estate is expensive

The final challenge everyone is faced with is that data center real estate is much more expensive than desktop real estate. And we're not just talking about the physical floor space. Power costs more because it has to be backed up, and the air is specially climate controlled. You pay more for MIPS on server-class hardware, and storage capacity, features, and IOPS all cost more.

Now you might say, "But the data center-based desktops (VDI or RDSH) have certain economies of scale, so while the servers and storage are more expensive, you also have more users to spread the cost." This is true. But come on—you can buy a desktop for $400 and a laptop for $500. It's really hard to beat that. (And $500 laptops work offline with great graphics and USB cameras.)

Actually, while we're talking about the costs of VDI, we should address our third fundamental myth of VDI:

Myth No. 3: VDI is Cheaper Than Traditional Desktops

A lot of people think that VDI is about saving money. But that's simply not true. Sure, VDI has a lot of advantages, but it typically ends up costing more money than traditional desktops. But that's okay! It's fine to spend more money for more features. This is the way the world works. More features = more money.

We often explain this in terms of cars. If you decide to replace an old junker car with a new one that has heated seats, GPS navigation, and computer-controlled automatic parallel parking, that new car will be more expensive than your old car. But that's okay because the new car has those awesome new features! So it's fine to spend more on the new car than the old car. And when it comes to VDI, it's totally okay to pay more for it than your traditional desktops, since VDI gives you great new features.

Now at this point you might be thinking that this is total hogwash—that "more money for more features" doesn't apply to computers, what with Moore's Law and all. But that's hogwash, too. Take Blackberries, for example. Giving your users Blackberries is more expensive than users without Blackberries. You have to buy the devices, the data plans, the Blackberry Enterprise Server, the licensing, the training, the support contracts—and all of those are additional costs you have for Blackberries that don't exist if you don't use Blackberries. But does that mean that no one uses Blackberries because they cost more? Of course not! IT folks recognize that even though having Blackberries costs more than not having them, having access to email anytime from anywhere is awesome and worth the money. So we pay more for the devices.

So why isn't the same true for VDI? What crazy world do we live in where VDI has to be cheaper than traditional desktops? Why the heck do we expect new features and higher availability and access from anywhere but then still expect all that new capability to be cheaper?!?! What kind of crazy, bizarro world is that?

An attempt to save money with VDI

While explaining this concept at an event last year, one of the attendees challenged us. He claimed that for his company, VDI was cheaper. He explained that right now they're spending $1,000 per desktop for new equipment every four years. If they went to VDI, they could buy $200 thin clients instead of $1,000 desktops. Then they could use some of the $800 saved per desktop to buy the back-end servers, storage, licenses, etc., for the complete environment, which he estimated at $500 per user. All in all, they're saving $200 per desktop by going to VDI.

At first you might think, "Okay, so for this guy, VDI is about saving money." But there are actually several problems with this example, and it turns out his alleged savings are total garbage.

First, you can buy PCs for $300 or $400. So we would argue that the best way for this guy to save money is to stop buying $1,000 PCs and to instead buy $400 PCs. Now you might argue that he actually needs $1,000 desktops. Maybe his users are "power users" and they actually need that much computer. Okay, fine. But if that's the case, there's no way that a $200 thin client powered by a $500 back-end VDI kit is going to come anywhere close to delivering the computing power and user experience he needs.

So in this guy's case, is he saving money with his new plan? Yes! But he's not saving money because he's going to VDI—he's saving money because he's drastically cutting down the amount of desktop computing that he's delivering to his users. And he can do that with the $300 PC route—he doesn't need VDI at all.

The real reason people "save" money with desktop virtualization

Ironically, people save money with desktop virtualization only because they use the technology to deliver an inferior desktop product when compared with their existing physical desktops.

We already talked about how sometimes people say, "We're going to VDI. That will be cheaper because we're going to have shared (and therefore locked-down) disk images, which means the users can't screw things up, and that will be cheaper to manage than the current Wild West world of personal images." Again, that's true. But the money savings comes from the fact that they're locking down their desktop images, not because they're using VDI. And again, if you just want to save money, simply lock down your desktops and skip VDI altogether.

To be clear: There are a lot of wonderful and perfectly valid reasons to use VDI. It's just that saving money is not one of them. And if you use VDI as your excuse to completely overhaul the way you deliver desktops, then it's the complete overhaul that's saving you money, not the actual VDI.

That said, you still hear plenty of people claiming that VDI saves money. Heck, there are even people who've done VDI who claim that they're doing it to save money. So how do we reconcile our dogmatic "VDI is not about saving money" with people's real world claims that it does? Simple: You can make the cost models "prove" whatever you want.

The truth about IT cost models

Whenever people justify moving to VDI as a way to save money, they produce some kind of cost model or analysis that quantifies the amount of money they hope to save with the new solution. Anyone who's been in the industry awhile has seen these cost models. Consultants have them. Vendors have them. Your boss makes them. They range in complexity from a few simple lines on a napkin to multi-page Excel workbooks that could make a mathematician's head spin. And while it's truly rare that a company makes technology decisions based solely on cost models, it's a safe bet that they play at least a little part in most IT decisions.

All that makes what we're about to say all the more scary: When people create cost models to justify their VDI projects, we absolutely 100% guarantee they can easily rig the results to ensure the model comes out in their favor. Every time. No problem.

It's possible to take the same situation—the same company with the same apps and users—and easily create two models: one that shows VDI is brilliant and one that shows it's stupid.

We're not trying to suggest that people lie with these things on purpose. Rather, it's a sort of cognitive bias where people use the cost models to "prove" what they believed all along. How is this possible? It's simple, actually. Here are eleven things that happen when people use cost models to prove their case.

1. Bundle in the "soft" costs

Adding soft costs to the model is the simplest way to get it to swing widely in one direction. (Remember, these techniques work in both directions and can be used to calculate the soft costs of expenses or savings.) By "soft costs" we're talking about the qualitative costs that affect a value to the company that can't be quantified with money. Common soft costs include things like employee productivity or user satisfaction.

Of course, since we're talking about cost models here, if the person creating the model wants to include soft costs, they have to quantify them in order to plug them into their spreadsheet. So how do they quantify stuff like this?

For user productivity, sometimes people think, "We get 3,000 help desk calls per year, and 15% are related to desktop support. If each help desk call costs us $200 (another easily manipulated, total B.S. made-up number), then we can save $90k (3,000*0.15*200) per year if we virtualize our desktops and eliminate those calls!" This is their basic level of soft-cost manipulation.

If they want to take that to the next level, they can toss in the productivity lost while the users are down. They might calculate that the average loaded cost of an employee is $50 per hour, so if desktop virtualization saves each of their 1,000 employees two hours per year, that's a $100k (1,000*2*50) yearly savings right there! (Of course it's not like the employees are really going to work two more hours each year with desktop virtualization. In the real world, they'd probably just stay late to make up the time they lost while waiting for their desktops to be fixed.)

The sky's the limit for exaggeration in the soft-cost areas, and people can add all sorts of things to the hourly loaded cost of an employee. Sure, taxes and benefits are easy. What about training, facilities, admin overhead, equipment, knowledge of their specific environment, and lost earnings potential?

2. Move trackable costs to non-tracked areas

The easiest way for people to deal with the pesky costs that keep breaking their model is to just get rid of them! (Which they can easily do by reallocating them to areas that are not tracked by their model.) Power and air conditioning are great examples of this. One argument for VDI is that it could lead to more people working from home. This, in turn, could mean fewer people working in the corporate offices, which leads to lower rent, electricity consumption, and heating and cooling costs—all of which result in money saved for the company.

Of course in the grand scheme of the world, this is actually less efficient, because now the company just has each employee paying for his or her own power, cooling, and heating. So really they're just transferring costs from something the company pays for to something employees pay for. (Yeah, it's more complex than that because you have to take commute times and distances into consideration, too, but we're choosing to ignore that since we're trying to prove a point. See Number 10 below.)

Advanced liars (err, cost analysis consultants) can combine this with Number 1 to assign a cost to the productivity lost by not having face-to-face meetings.

3. If they can't prove it, they'll abuse it

A lot of people try to claim that VDI is more "green" (in the environmentally friendly sense of the word) than traditional computing, claiming that thin clients might consume 25 watts while traditional desktops are at 400 watts. But what the people saying this don't say (or don't know) is that the wattage a device is rated for does not mean it consumes that many watts at all times—it's simply the maximum number of watts that the thing can take before it blows up. So just because a server has two 800-watt power supplies doesn't mean it's actually consuming 1,600 watts whenever it's powered on. The actual consumption will vary based on how much memory is installed, how fast the processors are, how many peripherals and drives are installed, and what the users are doing on it.

But how do the people building the cost model know how much power each server is consuming at any given moment? Sure, some servers have instrumentation on this, and some power systems provide this data, but most don't. And most people don't even know about the wattage thing. So if someone is trying to kill new servers because they consume too much power, they'll usually just make up the number they use to calculate their per-hour operating costs. If they're wrong in the end, who will ever know? It's not like their facilities department is going to catch them later on.

This is different than the B.S. soft costs from Number 1 or the real hard costs that can be transferred out of an organization (Number 2). This is all about hard costs that they know are real but that they can't actually measure. So they toss 'em in!

4. Justify the savings of features they know they'll never use

Cost models are complex formulas made up of many components—some more easily justified than others. ("How much does this server cost and how many users can it support?" is more universally accepted than "How much increased productivity will we get from happy users?") But what if the person creating the cost model has "real" data that hurts them? No problem! If they can find other data that helps their cause, they'll put it in their cost model, even if they know it will never apply to their environment. The more universally accepted the data, the better!

Does their hypervisor allow them to overcommit their physical memory across multiple virtual machines? Great! They'll build it into the cost model, even though they know there's no way they'd ever do that in production!

Does the protocol they want to use consume half the bandwidth of a competitor's product they don't want to use? Fantastic! Put that into their model, even if they have a LAN environment with unlimited bandwidth.

5. Reframe the conversation

Remember that even though we're talking about cost models, "cost" is only part of the equation. In addition to talking about cost and total cost of ownership, people are talking about things like the return on investment. So maybe something is more expensive, but it's worth it because they get more features. (We're one of these people, since we spent a bunch of pages talking about that exact same thing earlier in this chapter.)

6. Fudge the current state

One thing that people don't always realize with cost models is that they usually compare two environments, typically a before and an after. It's the after environment that gets most of the focus, since that's the part after they have VDI and after they buy all their new servers. But remember that the after part is worthless without the context of the before. The people signing the check for the VDI project don't really care what the after number looks like; rather, they care about how the after number compares to the before. So if the people creating the cost model get stuck with their after number, they can just take a break and look at the before (or current) environment.

If the person creating the cost analysis thinks that this VDI thing is crazy but they can't get the model to show it quantitatively, they can apply these same techniques to their current state to make it look really cheap (which will in turn make the after look extra bad)! And of course if they want to make VDI look good, they just load up their current state to really maximize the cost savings of going to VDI.

Messing with the current state is so easy and can so drastically affect the outcome that it's almost cheating!

7. Ignore the implementation efforts

When thinking about VDI, there's so much focus on what the environment will look like once the project is done. But the actual project that migrates from the current to the virtual desktop environment can be huge. Not only does the project team have to figure out what hardware they want and which products they want to use, but they also have to determine how they're migrating their users, how they're going to approach virtualizing all the applications, how they're going to migrate the profiles, etc. And of course there's user training, all the effort of taking away the users' admin rights, explaining to users that they can't use their webcams on their thin clients, etc. All of that takes a lot of work. But in cases where people are trying to justify how great VDI is, maybe they don't mention any of this in their cost model?

7a. Include the implementation efforts

Of course there's a flip side to the previous technique—if someone wants to kill a project, they can also include the implementation efforts to make things look dire. (And remember, when they're including them, they can apply many of the other techniques outlined here.)

8. Move from high-end to low-end

This is something that was covered in the example about the guy who went from $1,000 desktops to $200 thin clients with VDI. His cost model showed that he was saving costs, but that's only because he moved from a local, high-end computing environment where his users had full control to a low-end shared environment that gives his users only a fraction of the computing power they had at their disposal prior.

We call this hacking the user experience (like hacking down a shrub, not like hacking a computer).

9. Complexify for impressive-ity

Most people don't like to admit that they don't understand something, especially if they can impress people by sounding like they know what they're talking about. So maybe a simple two-line cost model wouldn't be taken seriously, but if they build a multi-page gigantic model to prove their case, people might think, "Oooohh! That looks impressive. It must be right!"

Actually, the vendors have already done this for us. Every desktop virtualization vendor has cost model generators or cost analyzers on their websites or available to their resellers that can "prove" how much money you can save with their product. And these things are definitely the result of rooms full of MBAs with too much spare time. But, hey, they come from the vendor and they're super complex, so they must be accurate!

10. Ignore data that doesn't support their views

If there's only one liar's technique you take away from this section, make it this: If a person creating a cost model ever finds data that doesn't support his or her view, they just ignore it!

Since there's no universally accepted list of what's appropriate to include in a cost model, it's a simple matter for them to just ignore the data that doesn't help their cause. That way they can build a strong model that supports their desired case while showing their company will clearly (and swiftly) go out of business if the company chooses a different VDI technology than what the person making the model wants.

Remember, figures lie and liars figure. So fire up Excel and get to it!

11. Tell them cost models are B.S.

If the person who created the cost model is ever in a situation where they're going to lose, where their model isn't proving the case that they want and the business is about to make a decision based on someone else's model that they don't agree with, they've got one Hail Mary option: They can tell everyone that cost models are B.S. It's easy to use the previous ten techniques to show why it's stupid to make a major technology decision based on something as easily manipulated as an IT cost model.

Even vendors try to fool people with cost models

Using cost models to justify cost savings of a particular solution is not limited to internal folks and IT consultants. The desktop virtualization software vendors themselves are possibly the worst offenders.

For example, VMware has given presentations at VMworld events where they specifically show how VDI is cheaper than traditional desktops. They'll highlight CapEx and OpEx and detail all the reasons customers can save money (both hard and soft costs) by going with VDI.

Unfortunately, these presentations are very one-sided, and if you look at their arguments critically, you see that their savings just aren't there. But every time they give that presentation, there are a few hundred more people in the world who think that VDI is cheaper. (So we feel like it's our job to get them all to "unlearn" that!)

Let's look at a few specific examples that VMware has used in the past:

Misleading Tactic No. 1: VMware compares VDI to traditional computing, yet ignores RDSH

VMware's whole presentation is basically a cost savings analysis of VDI over traditional fat-client computing. The problem is that for every point made in the pro-VDI category, the exact same point could have been made in a pro-RDSH category. (So really

VMware was sharing the advantages of having a desktop in the data center.) So even if the savings they outline are true, customers could save even more money by going to RDSH instead of VDI. And sure, there are certain cases where VDI is needed and RDSH won't work, but the case studies VMware presents aren't those kind of cases. RDSH would have worked fine for them and would have been much cheaper than VDI.

Misleading Tactic No. 2: VMware assumes all apps will work with ThinApp

Another component of the VMware VDI solution is the app virtualization package ThinApp. The whole cost analysis that VMware shows is based on replacing your old fat desktops with VDI-based ones.

First they explain the cost and management savings of using a single shared master disk for all your users, and then they explain that you can use ThinApp to virtualize all of your applications. But they never mention that ThinApp can't virtualize 100% of your applications. Sure, it can do most of them. But it can't do 100%. (No app virtualization product can.) So what happens when you decide to implement a VMware VDI solution and you build your whole cost analysis model around getting rid of supporting your desktop and app issues and everything, but then you learn that you can't put all of your apps into ThinApp? Now you've got two choices:

- Install the apps natively into the VMs. This would work, but now you break your master disk savings, since the apps would either (a) be installed for all users in the master image, (b) be installed for each user into their delta differential files, or (c) you'd need to have multiple master images. Either way, you destroy your cost savings model and now you're dealing with departmental images and app compatibility issues just like before.

- Install the apps onto the local traditional desktop clients. But now you have a major user experience problem, since VMware View only runs in remote desktop mode (i.e., no published apps): Your users have to switch back and forth between two desktops, and you'd have profile sync issues and all sorts of problems. And of course you'd still have to support local desktops, again completely destroying your cost savings model because you're not removing any costs.

Lots of Places Where VDI Is Awesome

You might think after reading all this that we really hate VDI. But, in fact, we love it! What we hate is when VDI is used where it doesn't make sense. In those cases—inevitably—the truth comes out (that VDI isn't right), but by that time, it's too late and the customer hates VDI. The problem isn't VDI, though; it's that the customer went to VDI where it doesn't make sense.

So we would say we hate when VDI is used where it doesn't make sense, but we don't hate VDI itself.

To that end, there are millions of users in the world who use VDI every day and where it makes a lot of sense. Now, keep in mind that there are more than 500 million corporate desktops in the world, so the percentage of users who use VDI is only maybe 1% or 2%. So we're not saying that VDI is ever going to be the majority. But there are a lot of people successfully using it today.

So where does VDI make sense? Here's how you figure out it.

VDI is about desktops in the data center

Fundamentally, VDI is about putting Windows desktops in the data center. As we mentioned previously, Microsoft RDSH is also about putting Windows desktops in the data center. So if you want to figure out where VDI makes sense, you first have to figure out if you have a certain population of users where it makes sense to put their desktops in the data center. Then (and only then) you can decide which flavor of desktops in the data center is right for them—VDI or RDSH.

So let's take a look at the advantages you get when you put a user's Windows desktop in the data center. (This is a subset of the "what was promised" with VDI list in the previous chapter. The difference here is that these are actual real advantages of desktops in the data center.)

Advantage No. 1: Centralized management

One of the tough things about managing traditional desktops and laptops is that users are scattered all over the place, which means the computers you have to manage are all over the place. Even if you have some kind of management tool like Microsoft SCCM or Altiris CMS, you still don't really know if all the computers will be on or if they can download the updates or if your scripts successfully ran.

So if it's your job to manage hundreds or thousands of desktops, what would you rather have: a thousand laptops scattered across who knows where, or a thousand VMs in the data center two floors down from you?

Note that data center-based desktops are easier to manage solely because they're physically located in a controlled location. It has nothing to do with sharing disk images or anything like that.

Advantage No. 2: Access from anywhere

Another problem with traditional desktops is that the Windows OS is installed on the physical desktop or laptop. So as long as the user is at that particular computer, no problem. But if you take the copy of Windows off of that computer and move it into a data center, the user can now access his or her entire Windows desktop environment almost instantly from any device.

Actually, if you move a user's desktop to the data center, that user can probably walk up to any Internet-connected device on the planet and be accessing their desktop in fewer than 100 keystrokes. Very cool!

This is great for people who use different computers. It's nice to know that no matter where you are or where you're going, you can access your desktop. It's nice that you can still get access to everything without having to go into an office or when you're stuck somewhere.

Advantage No. 3: Consistent performance

One of the big reasons data center-based Windows desktops became popular (via SBC in the 1990s) was because they provided a great way for fat client/server apps to run over slow WAN connections. Without Terminal Server, an application client would be installed on a desktop in some faraway location and performance would be horribly slow. To remedy this, IT admins installed Terminal Servers (or WinFrame servers) in the data center, which ran the app clients locally. That way, the app could run at full speed, since it was communicating with its back end across a fast network. Sure, the remoting protocol traffic had to traverse the slow WAN, but that traffic was generally a lot more tolerant of the slow network, and the user was able to get a decent experience.

And now, 15-plus years later, that's still a great reason for putting desktops in the data center. Users know that their applications are running at full speed, and they know their applications will keep running even if their devices become disconnected or have a problem. And that's the real advantage. Sure, there may be times when the network is slow and the remote desktop is hard to use, but that's a trade-off for knowing that the desktop is always running at full speed in a stable location.

Advantage No. 4: Increased security

The final great reason that people like to run their desktops in the data center is the potential for better security, since all application execution, data, and files are in the data center. If a user loses a laptop, they don't have to worry about encryption or backup or anything—there's no data on it.

The same is true for the network. Since the remoting protocols simply transmit graphical screen elements instead of actual files, there's nothing to intercept on the network.

In fact, one of the early wins for VDI was financial firms that took a "security at any cost" position. And based on what we've covered so far in this chapter, that should make sense. They wanted the absolute maximum security possible for their desktops (which was VDI), and they didn't care about how much it cost.

Real-World VDI Adoption

So now that we've really dug into the reality of VDI, including where it works, where it doesn't, and some of the challenges it faces, let's take a look at how people are using VDI in the real world. (And, just as importantly, scenarios where people are not using VDI in the real world.)

If VDI is so great, why aren't you using it?

Before we dig into how people are using VDI, are you using VDI? We don't mean your users. We mean "you" as in "you personally." Why aren't you *personally* using VDI? Is it because you're a road warrior? Because you need your VMs locally? Because you're a Mac user? Because you need graphically intense applications? Because you don't want to cede control? Because you hate your boss?

It's funny how on the one hand we hear about how awesome VDI is and on the other we trip over ourselves to find reasons why VDI is not right for us. We're all VDI NIMBYs!

Everywhere we go in this industry—conferences, vendor offices, our offices—all we see are laptops. And these laptop users sure aren't using VDI. We don't see people at Citrix, Quest, Microsoft, or VMware using VDI. Sure, they'll tell you that there's a corporate VDI environment they can connect to if they want, but if you push them, you learn it's something that they used twice when it first came out and not since.

And this is what VDI is competing against. Windows 7 installed locally on a laptop is really good! And VDI is not going to beat it anytime soon. Not this year. Not next year. Not in five years.

The collected masses aren't stupid. If VDI were so cheap, convenient, manageable, flexible, and wonderful, everyone would be using it. But VDI is a niche.

VMware's Own Internal Use Confirms VDI Is a Niche

As we've already said, VMware deserves credit for inventing VDI in the context that we're talking about it in this book. And we know they have an internal deployment of View that's available to all their users. But we feel like every VMware employee we meet has a laptop running a desktop locally.

We actually talked to VMware's PR people about this recently. At the time, VMware had 10,400 employees. Of that group, about one-third of them use VDI-based virtual desktops as their primary production work desktops. About 1,000 of them use a thin-client device as their only corporate-issued client device.

The remaining employees have access to a View desktop, which many of them use to complement their existing traditional laptop for things like occasional remote access, hotel cubes with thin clients, conference rooms via iPads, etc.

So here you have the company that invented VDI and only one-third of their employees are using it. Some people say, "Hey, the fact that VMware only has a minority of users on VDI shows how bad VDI is." But we don't think that's what it means at all. Instead, we believe this is saying, "VMware is acting smart and rationally here. They have this VDI technology which makes sense in some use cases, and instead of shoving VDI down everyone's throat regardless of whether it makes sense or not, they're only using it where it makes sense and allowing other users to use traditional laptops."

There's no better way to say it. VDI is not right for every use case. It's amazing where it makes sense. But, unfortunately, it's been foisted onto many people who don't want it.

In the next chapter, we're going to take a closer look at companies' VDI projects to see where they get stuck and exactly why they don't work. Then in Chapter 5, we'll look at types of desktop virtualization that are alternatives to VDI.

Chapter 4

Why Do VDI Projects Fail?

Regardless of the myths and challenges of VDI that we outlined in the previous chapter, a lot of people have still pushed ahead with VDI. Have they been successful? Sometimes. (And in the last chapter, we looked at some of the scenarios where VDI makes sense.) But more often than not, these VDI projects have failed in one way or another. Some were spectacular failures, while others never really met expectations.

So what happened? What went wrong? Presumably these projects were all led by smart people who knew their stuff. In this chapter, we're going to dig into the details of how and why people have failed with VDI.

By the way, let's take another moment to remind you that we're not VDI haters. We actually love VDI! (Seriously!) What we don't like is when VDI gets a bad name when it fails because people try to use it for the wrong reasons. So we're hoping that by sharing real-world examples of how other people have failed with VDI, you'll be able to avoid these situations and (1) only use VDI where it makes sense, and (2) be very successful with it!

Major VDI Failures

Some VDI initiatives fail in such big ways that entire projects are jeopardized or canceled outright. The only things that can prevent this are good planning and self-awareness.

Major Failure No. 1: Thinking that VDI is the same as server virtualization

Remember we mentioned in Chapter 1 that VMware more or less invented the VDI space because they'd already convinced everyone to virtualize their servers and they needed something else to sell? And remember how VMware could get in front of any CIO in the world to preach the desktop virtualization message? Organizations were quick to jump on board because, after all, they'd already done server virtualization. So how hard could it be to do desktops? This is also why, when most people hear the term "desktop virtualization," they instantly think of VDI. (And it's why we called this book "The VDI Delusion" instead of "The Desktop Virtualization Delusion.") The problem is that, across the board, server virtualization couldn't be more different than desktop virtualization. (Really, it's unfortunate that just because "virtualization" is used in the term "desktop virtualization," people automatically think it's the same as server virtualization.)

RELATIVE COMPLEXITY OF VIRTUALIZATION

DESKTOPS

SERVERS

(Scientific-looking graph)

As we outlined in Chapter 1, the reason server virtualization took off was because companies had all these physical computers in one room (the data center) that were all running at about 20% utilization. So consolidating those underutilized servers with server virtualization made sense. When it came to desktops, people thought, "Hey, our desktops are also running at a very low average utilization, so let's consolidate those too!"

While that was a nice thought, the key difference is that servers were already in the data center to begin with, so consolidating them meant that each server instance just moved a few shelves over once it became a VM. But for desktops, they had to be moved from out in the wild into the data center, and that's just not the same thing.

The other big difference is that virtualizing a server starts with something you already know (how busy that server is in that data center). It's easy to be confident in consolidating those servers because the users aren't going to change how they use the server after it's been virtualized. But when it comes to desktops, how do you know how busy the users are going to be? If you take a desktop and move it into the data center, will the user use it more? Or less? Do you even know how much they used their desktops before you wanted to move them into the data center?

The final big difference between server virtualization and desktop virtualization is that users plug all sorts of different peripherals into their desktops. In a traditional desktop environment, a user can plug in a USB drive or camera and it will work fine. In a VDI desktop environment, that user plugs the device into their client, but their copy of Windows that's running in the data center has to connect via USB over the network to access that device. What will that experience be like?

You can't take for granted the fact that you successfully implemented server virtualization in your organization. So did everyone else. You have to understand that moving from physical servers to virtual servers was a small evolutionary change, but moving from physical desktops to virtual desktops is a huge revolutionary change.

Major Failure No. 2: Doing too much at once

Another major failure that we touched on in the previous chapter comes when companies try to do too much at once. The biggest example of this is moving from a traditional environment where every PC is different to a VDI environment where all the users are sharing the same base image. People don't appreciate how hard it is to move from persistent to shared images.

The failure occurs as people get into the projects and realize that shared images aren't going to work for them. Then they say, "Okay, this VDI project failed." But if they had spent a few years getting their traditional PC environment working with shared images first, the move to VDI wouldn't have been too harsh. Or they could move into VDI with persistent images first and then pursue shared images later. Either one of those is fine. But changing desktop image type and moving to VDI at the same time—that's just too much.

The same thing can happen with OS and software versions. If you have Windows XP on traditional PCs and then you decide you want to move to Windows 7 and VDI at the same time, there are plenty of stories about companies that failed because they didn't get the Windows 7 part right (usually due to application compatibility and user profile issues). Or they spent so much effort trying to get the Windows 7 part right, they never gave the VDI engineering enough focus to succeed.

In all those cases, they would have been better off going from physical Windows XP to VDI Windows XP and then to Windows 7, or first implementing Windows 7 on their physical PCs and then doing VDI as a separate project after that.

Major Failure No. 3: Thinking VDI is cheaper than traditional desktops

We don't have to go into the details of why VDI isn't cheaper than traditional desktops here since we covered it in the last chapter, but even if you're on board with that as a concept, you're probably still wondering how a lack of cost savings can directly lead a VDI project to fail. There are several ways, actually.

First, if the people who justified the VDI project in the first place based their thinking on saving money, you're going to have a major problem when they're forced to try to show they've achieved their savings goals with your VDI project. For example, if you initially try VDI with a shared disk model and that doesn't work, it may turn out that your VDI could be wildly successful for you if you simply switch to a persistent disk model. But if you didn't build those additional storage costs into your model, it might not be possible to switch, and your project will fail.

The same is true if you have to cut corners to justify your cost savings. Maybe you thought, "Okay, we want to do VDI, but to justify the cost, we can only afford 10,000 IOPS for our 500 users." This would lead to major performance problems that could kill your project.

VDI, as we learned, is not about saving money. VDI is about satisfying technology or operational goals, like the ability for users to have a full desktop from anywhere, DWI (Doctors with iPads), disaster recovery, escaping the PC refresh cycle, and so on. If you think VDI is just about saving money, there's a good chance that your project will fail.

Major Failure No. 4: Not knowing why you're doing VDI in the first place

If you're thinking about VDI, are you able to explain why? Because if any of the following reasons are at the top of your list, you're probably setting yourself up for VDI project failure:

- It's sexy, and it looks like everyone else is doing it.

- _____ (insert vendor name here) gave us the licenses along with some other big purchase.

- My buddy at another company did it, so I'll just take their plan.

- It's just like server virtualization! (See above, and shame on you for skipping ahead if you have to look back.)

- I was told to do desktop virtualization, and this is it, right?

- I'm in charge of our virtual environment, so if we can expand that to include desktops, I am in charge of a whole lot more.

It's hard to be successful with any project if you don't have specific goals set ahead of time. With VDI, it's even more critical, since VDI affects many users and it's such a fundamental change from the world of traditional PCs. If you don't have an iron-clad reason for needing VDI, there's almost no chance that you'll be able to be successful with it.

If you don't have an iron-clad reason, by the way, all is not lost. In the next chapter, we'll look at several other technologies that are other types of desktop virtualization. And if you want to know some good reasons to use VDI in the first place, we'll cover those in Chapter 6.

Major Failure No. 5: Underestimating how critical the network is for VDI

Remember that when you use VDI, your users' desktops run in the data center, yet the devices they connect from are on users' desks or at their homes. This means that every mouse movement, key press, and click has to be remotely transmitted to your data center, and every pixel that changes on the Windows desktop has to be broadcast down to the user. This is done via a remoting protocol (which varies depending on which VDI product you use, but could be VMware PCoIP, Citrix HDX, or Microsoft RemoteFX).

There are two things to keep in mind when determining how remoting protocols will affect your project. First, no matter how good your network is, remoting Windows will not be as good as Windows running locally. Second, if you don't believe this, your project will probably fail.

While the details of remoting protocol performance are beyond the scope of this book (though it's a topic we discuss often on BrianMadden.com), just remember that user experience is king, so you have to be sure that your network and your VDI product's remoting protocol can actually meet your users' expectations. All we can say here is test, test, test. Don't think that your experience using Citrix for ten years to deliver a simple forms-based Windows app means you know how to deliver 1900x1200, multi-display, 3-D Aero video apps to users with webcams and USB sticks connecting from thin clients over a WAN.

Major Failure No. 6: Thinking that desktop virtualization is only VDI

If you ask most IT professionals to explain what desktop virtualization is, they'll describe a scenario where a user connects to a VM in a remote data center running a Windows desktop OS. (In other words, they'll describe VDI.) While VDI is certainly a type of desktop virtualization, it's not the only type. A lot of VDI projects fail simply because the company chose VDI when RDSH, client-based VMs, or app virtualization would have been a more appropriate approach. (We'll dig into all of these "other" forms of desktop virtualization in the next chapter.)

Major Failure No. 7: Turf wars and career advancements

VDI projects cross a whole bunch of boundaries within the IT department. Not only does this include the desktop and server teams, but virtualization administration, networking, security, storage, application support, mobile device management—the list goes on and on.

The challenge is that there's a sort of social hierarchy within every IT department, and in most cases, even though the groups are different, the groups higher up on the list think they know more than the lower groups. While this hierarchy differs from company to company, it usually looks something like this:

1. CIO
2. Security
3. Virtualization
4. Networking
5. Server
6. Storage
7. Desktop architect
8. App support
9. PC tech
10. Help desk
11. Pigeons in the cafeteria
12. Mac people

So looking at this hierarchy, who's going to manage your VDI environment? What teams will be involved? Will one group be responsible for the entire solution, including hardware, networking, and software, or is it broken up?

As we mentioned earlier in this chapter, there is usually a very fine line between the desktop team and the server team in an organization. In many companies, there's also a separate network team and storage team. Successful VDI projects require one of two things:

- Total cooperation between all of these teams
- Total autonomy for a select group of people with a very large skill set

The problem is that politics, agendas, and general infighting can disrupt either of those. With so many critical resources at stake, the ability to communicate and control them in near-real time is critical, and the more red tape there is, the worse the experience will be for the users and the organization as a whole.

Some organizations designate the server team to be in charge of the physical hardware and the hypervisor, leaving the desktop team in charge of the virtual machines and everything inside them. This kind of situation can work well in organizations with good communication and mutual respect, but that arrangement doesn't come along every day.

Other companies have designated a certain group of people as sort of the virtualization team. The people in these groups are often good at all areas necessary for day-to-day operations of server and desktop virtualization, but people with that broad of a skill set are often hard to come by (and certainly not cheaply).

Beyond the technical operations, though, are the business drivers. In many organizations, IT is seen as a soul-sucking money pit by higher ups that are less technical. Corporate buy-in by leadership is critical, and if someone in power isn't sold on the concept, they could make it very difficult. Imagine if you had total cooperation from the server, desktop, and storage teams, but not the network team.

Finally, don't forget that virtualization is sexy, and a lot of people love the concept of VDI without really thinking about the impact or even understanding what exactly it is. All they know is if they can get the VDI project under their control, that's an opportunity to advance their own career. (Talk about doing VDI for the wrong reasons!)

We know that you don't need us going on and on about how people and politics can derail a project before it even gets started. Just consider all the different people that need to be involved in a VDI project before the project starts, then get them on board.

Many Minor VDI Failures

The minor failures that we see affecting VDI projects amount to ones that, if left alone, could probably be overcome by perseverance, technology, or money. While they might not kill a VDI project outright, they can certainly screw up its degree of success.

Minor Failure No. 1: Not understanding Microsoft licensing

There's an axiom in our industry that goes something like this: *If you speak to ten different people at Microsoft about how VDI licensing works, you'll get eleven different answers.*

It's completely ridiculous that we haven't gotten this figured out, but the reality of our world is that Microsoft licensing can be a reason that VDI projects stall or fail. The devil, as they say, is in the details.

Some companies move to a VDI project blissfully unaware that anything is different when it comes to licensing Windows desktops delivered via VDI. Others think they're doing the right thing by having RDS CALs for use with VDI. They'd all be wrong, of course, but finding the real solution proves to be exceptionally difficult.

Microsoft licenses VDI desktops differently than traditional desktops or RDSH desktops. To make matters worse, the license names and usage rules tend to change over time. Here's what's true at the time of this writing:

Software Assurance and VDA

You probably know that Software Assurance (SA) entitles the users of devices initially purchased with Windows (and renewed yearly) to certain privileges. Having SA on a device, for example, means you can be upgraded to the latest version of Windows without having to purchase it again. It also means that you are entitled to use Windows desktops hosted in the data center via VDI for no extra cost. There's more, but that's the gist of it as it pertains to desktop virtualization.

There's a catch, though, when a user's VDI client device is not entitled to SA. This could be for a number of reasons:

- SA expired
- The user never bought SA to begin with
- The device isn't able to run Windows (i.e., it's a thin client or iPad)

If the device you're using doesn't have SA, then you need to purchase a different Microsoft license, called a "VDA" license. VDA grants you the same VDI rights as SA, but none of the other rights (upgrades, for example). VDA is also at per-year pricing and retails at around $100 a device per year.

Device versus user licenses?

Everything we've mentioned so far about VDI licensing has been about client device-specific licenses. If you think this is a nightmare because most other products are licensed per named user or per concurrent user, we agree.

To add salt to the wound, even if you have VDA or SA on your main client device at the office, your users are technically not allowed to access their virtual desktop from, say, a thin client or iPad without another VDA license. (We say "technically" because Microsoft doesn't actually have a way of enforcing this rule other than a legal department that is quite possibly larger than your entire company.)

There's an exception to this second license requirement for home scenarios with something called Extended Roaming Rights

(ERR). ERR lets users access their Windows VDI desktops from devices without VDA or SA as long as their primary device back in the office has SA or VDA. The catch with ERR is that it doesn't apply to devices that are physically used in the office. So a user can use their iPad at home no problem, but if they bring it into the office, they require a separate VDA license for it. Yikes!

What about Microsoft Office?

Microsoft Office is also licensed on a per-device basis, so technically (there's that word again, like a drinking game) any device used to access Office via VDI needs its own license. (This is also something that Microsoft can't enforce within Office itself, but you should consider their entire skyscraper full of lawyers when determining whether you'll comply.)

Office licenses are also able to receive SA benefits, though, so they also have ERR privileges. The same restrictions as Windows apply though, so while Office ERR helps out the users who only work from home and from a single client device in the office, it doesn't help those who have a tablet to take into conference rooms.

Is there any way to possibly get this right?

If you think this sounds crazy, you're not alone. Windows licensing is one of the most hated aspects of VDI, but because Windows applications dominate most corporate environments, there really isn't any alternative other than to make sure you understand the licenses and pay up.

Actually, we should say there isn't really any alternative if you have to use VDI. If you can use RDSH, great. RDSH has its own Client Access Licenses (CALs) that are not at all related to SA or VDA. RDS CALs can be purchased per device or per user, and they're perpetual, which means that you buy them once and you're finished. There are no device restrictions, and no on-/off-premises discussions. The biggest problem is that you're still bound by the application-specific licensing, so Office technically (drink!) needs to be licensed for each device being used.

As far as we're concerned, the right way to do this is to call the Microsoft rep who handles your Enterprise Agreement, get meticulously documented information, and follow it as closely as you can while keeping a clear conscience. We call this the "straight-face test." If you can relay your strategy to someone of importance without wincing, smiling, or looking shifty, then it's probably okay.

The worst thing that can happen is to get your VDI project under way and then find out later on that you have to buy thousands of dollars' worth of VDA licenses.

Minor Failure No. 2: Picking the wrong product for the wrong reason

There are several major vendors (Citrix, Microsoft, Quest, VMware) and over a hundred minor ones that make products to run and support your VDI environment. They all have different features, capabilities, and ways of working. If you look at your specific environment, some of these products are more right for you than others. So which product should you choose?

We can't give you a definitive recommendation about which one is best here, because what's best for you depends on your use case and your needs. What we can tell you is that plenty of VDI projects have failed simply because the companies picked a product that wasn't right for them.

We can spend all day coming up with reasons not to pick products. For example, a lot of people choose VMware View for their VDI environment simply because they also use VMware for their server virtualization platform. But as we said in the beginning of this chapter, server virtualization is not the same thing as desktop virtualization, so why would you automatically pick the vendor for one based on the other? Do you automatically choose Dell laptops just because you have Dell servers? Does your company automatically buy Volvo cars for employees because their delivery trucks are Volvo? Don't get us wrong: VMware View is a fine product, but so are Citrix XenDesktop, Quest vWorkspace, and Microsoft's own VDI suite. (Okay, maybe not Microsoft's.) Do you really want to base your decision on how thousands of users get their desktops every day on the fact that some server engineer bought VMware back in 2004? (By the way, remember you can still use VMware vSphere as the hypervisor for your project and then choose a different desktop virtualization platform to go on top of it.)

Other examples of picking the wrong product come from vendors giving you free licenses. Maybe VMware throws in 500 View licenses with your vSphere enterprise agreement renewal, or maybe Citrix tells you that if you renew your XenApp subscription, they'll give you access to XenDesktop for free. While these are all nice gestures, we wouldn't want to make an enterprise platform decision based on a freebie from a sales rep.

Or maybe one vendor talks about how much simpler their product is to install than the others, or about how fast they can provision virtual machines to users. These are very concrete numbers that are very easy to back up with data, but ultimately you have to ask yourself whether it matters if it takes an extra day to stand up a solution or a few extra hours to automatically provision your desktops. Once the system is up and running, do you care?

Minor Failure No. 3: Not having the technical skills to pull it off

VDI is complex—let's just get that out there now. We're not saying it's not worth doing, but you're taking your existing desktops, adding in some new technology, and fundamentally changing the way you deliver them. Now you have to know about servers and storage and networks and VPNs and thin clients and protocols—plus you still need to know about Windows desktop applications and user profiles and printing and...

We can say with extreme confidence that plenty of real-world VDI deployments have failed for the simple reason that the people who designed and operate them have no idea what the heck they're doing. This is sort of related to some of the other reasons for failure that we mentioned before. Some people think, "I am the virtualization expert here, so I will design the VDI environment." Then that project fails because that virtualization expert didn't read up on desktop virtualization and instead just copied the server environment.

Also, plenty of people fail at VDI because they think, "I've been using Citrix since the 1990s, so I'm an expert on data center hosted desktops," or "I'm an expert with thin clients and remoting protocols, so this is no different." The problem with VDI is that since it's the entire desktop, everything has to work. VDI isn't some simple forms-based business app delivered seamlessly; it's about a full desktop with multiple huge monitors, including everything the user needs, like video conferencing, graphics, YouTube, and user-installed apps.

Server virtualization skills from the 2000s and the Citrix skills from the 1990s are both great starting points for your VDI skills of today, but you're not automatically there just because of your background. VDI requires VDI-specific skills.

Minor Failure No. 4: Thinking VDI will solve the "tablet problem"

How many iPads is Apple selling a year now? 50 million or something? (Does the exact number even matter? Let's just say it's a lot.) Subsequently, everyone is scrambling to try to figure out how they're going to support these things (or even if they'll support them).

So it comes as no surprise that every vendor that sells anything even remotely related to iPads is saying they can help. A lot of VDI vendors do the same thing when it comes to tablets. "Hey," they'll say, "with VDI you can deliver your entire enterprise desktop to your tablet users!"

This is true. However, using a Windows desktop that was meant for a keyboard and mouse isn't exactly a great experience on a tablet. Of course, if you already have VDI, sure, go ahead and make it available to your tablet users. Why not, right? It doesn't really cost you anything extra, so go for it. But delivering a corporate Windows desktop to your tablet users isn't going to satiate their desire for real touch-based tablet apps.

So if you can do it, go for it. But if you're doing VDI as a way of dealing with tablet users, you're going to fail.

Minor Failure No. 5: Buying for the future

When you were twenty-two years old and had no spouse and no kids, did you buy a minivan because you expected to have a family someday? Heck no. If you had, that minivan would be old when you needed it in five or ten years, and it's always possible that you'd never need a minivan anyway.

The same holds true for VDI. If it doesn't meet your current needs, don't buy it thinking it will in the future. Instead, focus on the solutions that do address your current needs. If you want VDI functionality but without the complexity, find the company with the solution you need that also works on traditional desktops. For instance, you don't need VDI to do layering (Wanova, MokaFive), disk encryption (BitLocker), user virtualization (AppSense, RES, Immidio, Scense, triCerat), or OS streaming (Citrix, Wyse, Dell, Lenovo).

Minor Failure No. 6: Moving bad habits to the new environment

There's a guy from our past—way back from the 1990s—whom we'll call Mr. Lesshon. Lesshon was a server guy, working on NetWare servers most of his life but also dabbling in Windows NT to the point of knowing more than the average IT pro. Unfortunately, his knowledge came from the desktop side.

Lesshon believed the best way to maintain proper functionality of the OS was to run a full ScanDisk or CHKDSK at every boot, regardless of the reason the machine was turned off in the first place. If Lesshon ever had a file on his laptop that we needed, we'd have to make the request in the morning and come back after lunch to see if his machine had booted yet.

This wouldn't have been a big deal if it only affected his machine, but the problem was that his same general belief made its way into the servers he managed. When tasked with standing up a Windows server at a company that only had one or two servers back then (so they did everything from file storage to DNS/DHCP/WINS), they needed a server to be backed up ASAP. Unfortunately, running CHKDSK slowed the process down. A lot. Customers weren't happy.

To us, this is a classic example of moving bad habits to the new environment. It was already not a very good practice, and evaluating it ahead of time before doing it in the data center would've saved a lot of headaches for Lesshon and his customers. The same holds true today in the context of desktop virtualization and VDI.

VDI and RDSH are concentrated desktop deployments. That means that you concentrate both the good and bad traits. When we were only using RDSH, this wasn't as big of a deal because we had to re-evaluate all of our applications and processes anyway as we moved to a shared image server OS. But with VDI, we're still talking about managing normal desktops that have simply changed form factor. While that's a liberating statement, it's often taken too far.

If your old habit was to give local users admin rights, for instance, and you continue doing that in your VDI environment, it will be hard to meet expectations like "better security" or "ease of management," since your users will be able to do the same crazy things as before.

Another good example is antivirus, which you have running full steam on every traditional desktop in your organization. If you continue that practice in your VDI desktops, you'll drive the storage system usage through the roof. This will either cause you to spend significantly more money on expensive storage to accommodate that (which would be bad) or to have terrible performance because you now have to support five times the IOPS you should be supporting.

The point here is that a desktop virtualization project is an excellent time to take a step back and look at the habits and processes that you and your department use in your daily life. Don't just assume that everything translates from one form factor to the other.

Minor Failure No. 7: Not doing a good assessment

One of the hardest things about VDI is doing a good assessment of how your users use their existing traditional desktops before they go to VDI. Too many people think that assessments are just about server sizing. They try to figure out how much CPU and memory and IOPS each user VM is going to need. While a poorly sized VDI server can certainly kill a VDI project, it's pretty easy to test and figure out what you're going to need ahead of time.

What's harder to figure out is what your users need outside of what you can see in Perfmon. For example, what USB devices do your users use? Sure, your VDI solution might have "USB support," but what does that mean? Does it support the whole stack? What happens if a user plugs in a USB stick full of music? Will reading those files from the remote VDI session crush the network and make everyone else's VDI performance go down the drain?

Another thing that surprises people who don't do assessments is that users often use applications that are critical to their business but that the central IT department doesn't know about. You might spend months planning your VDI environment with your shared images and virtual apps, and then when you cut over your users, you hear, "Hey, where's our such-and-such application?" You're confused because you never heard of it and so it's not in the image, and they say, "Yeah, we just went out and got it on our own. Our business unit owner approved it, and without it we can't do our jobs." And just like that, the project is halted.

Fortunately, there are several products on the market that you can use to perform these assessments. (Take a look at the products from Lakeside Software, Liquidware Labs, and Centrix Software.) They all enable you to analyze what your pre-VDI traditional desktop users do, and from there you can make smart decisions about what you need to support and if your users can even use VDI.

Minor Failure No. 8: Not knowing when to stop

We believe that almost every company in the world with over fifty users probably has a need for VDI somewhere. It might only be for 5% or 10% of your users, but it's probably something. The problem is that it's human nature to take comfort in what you know. (VMware took comfort in VMs and invented VDI and hypervisors for phones.) But this tendency can actually come back to hurt people.

Imagine you're at a company with 2,000 employees and fifty users of VDI. You probably picked the "right" users for VDI. They're happy, you're happy, the vendors are happy—VDI is great for you. Unfortunately, a lot of people see that and think, "Okay, now let's grow our fifty-user VDI environment to 200 users." But are there really another 150 users in your company who should be using VDI? (If so, wouldn't they have been using VDI already?)

This is a big problem we see all over the place. The first set of VDI users is great, but then the company hurts themselves when they try to grow VDI to more users where it doesn't make as much sense. Inevitably, people forget that VDI used to be good and now think that VDI stinks because none of the new users like it.

Bonus: Why VDI Projects Get Stuck in Pilot

So far this chapter has been about why VDI projects fail. One way they fail is they get built and users don't like them. Another way is that VDI gets put into pilot, but for one reason or another, it never grows or is never picked up from there. So in addition to all the above reasons that VDI fails, here are three reasons that sometimes cause VDI projects to get stuck in pilot forever.

Using old hardware

It seems like a lot of test labs are made up of old equipment and decommissioned servers. While this is fine for learning and playing, there's no way you can assume the user experience of VDI on old hardware will match up to what it would be like with new hardware. (Actually, even if you have new hardware, if it's not the exact hardware you're going to use for your production environment, you can't assume the same user experience on both.)

Some people think, "Well, let's at least see what the remoting protocol will be like on the old hardware, because bandwidth is bandwidth, right?" Unfortunately, even this doesn't work. Today's remoting protocols can leverage special tricks with certain CPU features and GPUs, meaning you can get a very different user experience—even with the same client, network, and back-end software—based solely on the hardware the back end is running on.

This is like when you're trying to introduce a friend to your favorite sport. Whether it's skiing or tennis or bike riding, if it's something you've been doing awhile, you probably have extra old or lower-end equipment your friend can borrow. So you're awesome at this sport using great equipment that works and keeps you comfortable, and your friend is a first-timer with old equipment. How likely is it that your friend will have a great experience? If you want to ensure their happiness, why not give them the best, newest equipment? The same goes for VDI.

Picking the easy people first

One technique that a lot of people try when it comes to piloting new technologies like VDI is to pick the simple users first. That way it's easier to show early success, especially as you're just getting your feet wet learning a new technology. While this is a great way to start, remember it means that you could potentially have a huge wall to climb to get from that group of users to your "real" users.

This is a tricky issue to balance, because we don't really love the alternative either. If you start with your most challenging users, sure, once you make them happy you can be confident that you can make anyone happy. But how long is that going to take? Three years? And now your other users are missing out on VDI that whole time?

We're not necessarily advocating that you don't start with your easy users. We're just saying that a lot of pilots don't grow because the people doing them knocked out the easy users first and got stuck. (Although in those cases, maybe that just means that the "pilot" users are actually the only production users they should have, in which case, we should congratulate them for finishing their rollout!)

No linear scalability

The final challenge with VDI pilots is that, in general, VDI doesn't have smooth, linear scalability. For example, we see all these numbers thrown around, like "VDI for $500 per user" or "VDI storage for $50 per user." While those numbers can certainly be true, keep in mind what they're saying.

When a vendor says "VDI for $500 a user," they really mean something like "fifty users of VDI for $25k." Does that mean you can do forty users for $20k? Nope. Forty users would still cost $25k. Does that mean you can do sixty users for $30k? Probably not. You might have to shell out another $25k for your next fifty users. So instead of saying "VDI for $500 a user," a more correct statement would be "$25k for each chunk of fifty users." See the difference?

If a single VDI server costs $9k and can support 100 users, you can only get that $90 per user if you have exactly 100 users. If you only have twenty-five users, you still need a $9k server, except now your cost is $360 per user. If you have 110 users, then you need two servers for $18k, meaning you're paying $163 per user.

When it comes to piloting VDI, we also see this "stair step" style scalability in our architectures. If you only have a few VDI host servers, you might be able to get away with local storage combined with some disk image streaming solution. That might work great for up to five servers, but beyond that, you might need to move to a real SAN. So your "jump" from five to six servers might cost $100k and require eight weeks of planning. Does that mean your old environment was not designed right? No! (Because it would be crazy to build the huge SAN for just a few servers.)

Just like many other things about business, as you grow, you're going to have to take some backward steps from time to time. Some people are afraid of these big jumps or that their boss will think they didn't design the environment properly, so their projects just stay stuck at the smaller size.

Summary

Well, that's depressing, isn't it? It seems like there are more ways to fail with VDI than there are to succeed! But if you keep these things in mind as you plan your project, you'll at least have a better chance than the poor people we learned these failures from. After all, there are millions of users in the world using VDI, many of them happily! So VDI can be wonderful.

We opened this chapter by reminding you that we're not VDI haters, and we want to remind you of that again here. Watching VDI fail spectacularly in so many ways reminds us that VDI is only a very small part of the larger desktop virtualization landscape, and that there are other ways to solve the problems that bring on the need for desktop virtualization in general. In the next chapter, we'll look at what other technologies make up the desktop virtualization space. From there, you can start to put together your Windows desktop virtualization strategy.

Chapter 5

Desktop Virtualization Is More Than VDI

Most people automatically assume "VDI" when they hear the words "desktop" and "virtualization" in the same sentence. But as we've hinted at previously, there are actually quite a few different technologies that are part of the overall desktop virtualization landscape, some of which have absolutely nothing to do with VDI.

For example, many of us have been delivering desktops from the data center for well over ten years with various Citrix products—all of which are perfectly valid types of desktop virtualization. We can also look at desktop virtualization as it extends beyond desktops in the data center, including application virtualization, user settings virtualization, client-side virtual machines, desktops as a service (DaaS), software as a service (SaaS), OS streaming, and even centrally managed traditional desktops. At its core, desktop virtualization isn't the name of a type of technology—it's the concept that connects your users to their Windows desktops and applications.

The Many Flavors of Desktop Virtualization

We've had many discussions over the years about what desktop virtualization is all about, and even today not everyone agrees on what should and shouldn't be considered desktop virtualization. But since this is our book, we get to go with our opinion.

This chart changes over time because the ways in which we manage Windows change. Back in 2007, we didn't have SaaS and DaaS on the list because we didn't consider them to be a big enough part of the picture. In 2003, we didn't have VDI, OS streaming, or client VMs on the list because those hadn't been invented yet. (Actually back then our diagram was just the letters "TS," which we circled in crayon.)

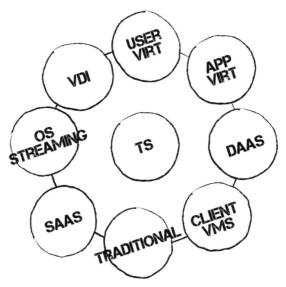

ALL OF DESKTOP VIRTUALIZATION

The world was simpler in those days, with a typical conversation between a reseller and customer going like this:

Reseller: Are you tired of using your Laplink cable to replicate desktops?

Customer: Yes, how did you know?

Reseller: How about replacing your desktops with something called a "thin client" that lasts for nine years and has no moving parts?

Customer: Whaaa??

Reseller: And what if these new thin clients just accessed a server in the server room that supported twenty people? And if you want to upgrade Office for twenty people, you just have to install it once.

Customer: Where do I sign?

Ah, the good old days! Let's start there, because as old as Terminal Services is, it's still, by far, the most used desktop virtualization solution with an estimated 100 million users worldwide.

Remote Desktop Session Host (Terminal Services)

Now called Remote Desktop Session Host (RDSH) or Remote Desktop Services (RDS), the technology was called Terminal Services (TS) for the bulk of its life prior to Windows Server 2008. That's why we still use the term today along with its analogue, server-based computing (SBC). (That's right, if you're keeping track, the acronyms RDSH, RDS, TS, and SBC all refer to this same concept. We use RDSH in this book unless we're specifically referring to an older version of the product.)

RDSH originated back in 1998 with Windows NT 4.0 Terminal Server Edition, which itself was the second iteration of the multi-user Windows platform originally invented by Citrix in the mid-1990s by modifying Windows NT 3.51 source code.

In today's world, RDSH is used to deliver session-based desktops and applications from the data center. Some people use the product by itself, while others (many others) use add-on products like Citrix XenApp or Quest vWorkspace.

The reason for the longevity of the product is that in the vast majority of situations that call for a data center hosted solution, RDSH-based solutions are the most cost-effective way to deploy desktops and applications. The density compared to VDI is unmatched, and after more than seventeen years of working within the confines of server-based desktops, we (as an industry) have gotten darned good at it!

Back in Chapter 3 we discussed the benefits of hosting your Windows desktops in the data center, including:

- Placing the three-tier applications closer to the data
- Efficient management of branch office infrastructure
- Publishing desktops and applications to devices that wouldn't otherwise support them
- Better security in that most of the data traversing the network is video data, keystrokes, and mouse clicks
- The ability to replace desktop computers with thin clients, which require less maintenance and have longer mean times between failure
- The ability to install and update applications in a central location
- Support for work-from-home programs
- Improved disaster recovery

Remember that these benefits apply to any instance where a Windows desktop is delivered via a remoting protocol. In other words, these benefits apply to both RDSH and VDI desktops. Because of this, people often wonder which option is better for them.

RDSH versus VDI

To be clear: When deciding whether RDSH or VDI is better for you, the first thing you have to determine is whether it makes sense to have your desktops in the data center. Then (and only then) do you decide which type of data center-based desktop you want—RDSH or VDI.

Assuming you've decided that data center-based desktops are right for you, how do you decide which one you should go with? Let's look at the advantages of each. (And one more time, just to be clear: If you're comparing RDSH or VDI to traditional desktops, then you'd have to include the advantages and disadvantages of data center-based desktops in general. But right now, we're just talking about the specific advantages that RDSH has over VDI and vice versa.)

Advantages of RDSH over VDI

The biggest advantage you get with RDSH over VDI is that it's cheaper. How much cheaper depends on all sorts of things, but generally you can expect to pay three or four times as much for data center hardware to run the same number of VDI users versus RDSH users. Why? It's simple: With VDI, each user has his or her own virtual machine, whereas with RDSH, you have lots of users sharing the same Windows Server virtual machine. So if you have 200 users, you'd have to run 200 virtual machines for VDI but only one for RDSH.

By the way, if you're surprised that we're mentioning a cost issue here after our whole diatribe against cost models back in Chapter 3, in this case we're not trying to analyze the overall value of the solution. Rather, we're just saying you will have to spend more money to support the same number of users if you use VDI. That is a fact.

Advantages of VDI over RDSH

So when it comes to options for hosting desktops in the data center, VDI is more expensive than RDSH. But as we discussed previously in the book, that's okay as long as it provides more capabilities, right? The good news is that VDI has lots of cool features that RDSH doesn't have.

First, VDI is nice because you're running the desktop version of the OS rather than the server version. So your users have the nice normal Windows desktop OS instead of a shared session on Windows Server. That means you can treat these users like "normal" users. The software installs in the same way, and everything works as expected. It's also easier for desktop admins to understand, since it's the normal Windows desktop OS.

Second, you get a lot more flexibility with VDI, since the VM "boundary" is around a single user, whereas with RDSH, you have lots of users on the same VM. So with VDI, you can do things like live migration to move single users from host to host. With RDSH, you can live-migrate an RDSH VM, but all of the users have to go along with it. You can't separate RDSH users who are on the same RDSH VM.

Why does this matter? One of the biggest problems that RDSH has always had (and still has) is what happens when two power-hungry users are unfortunate enough to coincidentally end up on the same RDSH host. Since the single RDSH server hosts multiple users, a single power user can take resources from other users. Microsoft has included CPU "throttling" technology ever since Windows 2008, which prevents a single user from negatively impacting the other users. But if you've got two power users on the same host, the CPU throttling would just knock them both down. So it's great that they're not impacting the other users, but they're also both essentially running at half speed. This is especially infuriating when you've got multiple RDSH hosts. You might have two users on the same host fighting each other for CPU, while right next to them you have another host that's wide open. But what's your option here? Do you want to send a message to one of the power users that says something like, "I'm sorry, you seem to be wanting to do a lot. Can you please log out and then connect again, and we'll hope that you're routed to a server with more availability?" But if you were using VDI, you could simply live-migrate the single power user's VM from one host to another and everything would be fine. The user wouldn't even know it happened. (Well, apart from the fact that everything would suddenly start running faster!)

Finally, when thinking about why VDI can be better than RDSH, consider that all your existing desktops and laptops run the regular Windows desktop OS. So if you want the advantages of data center-based desktops, you don't have to fundamentally change the way you do everything, like you would if you went to RDSH. With VDI, you can simply set up your Windows desktop environment so that it's 100% identical to your existing physical desktop environment, with the only change being that the desktops are running in the data center instead of on users' desks. Heck, with personal disk images and VDI, you could migrate from a physical desktop environment to a virtual desktop environment in a single weekend!

Client-Based Virtual Machines (Client Hypervisors)

Another type of desktop virtualization on the market today is known as the client-based virtual machine, or client hypervisor. Client-based virtual machines are a bit of an odd animal and have been around in one form or another for longer than you might think. In fact, VMware Workstation (a client-based virtual machine) predates any VMware server product by two years! For the vast majority of that time, though, client-based virtual machines were only found on admins' desktops and not used for any "normal" users. That started to change in the late 2000s, and as the industry looked for ways to grow the use of hypervisors beyond servers, the enterprise client-based virtual machine was born.

There are two kinds of client-based virtual machines, conveniently known as Type 1 and Type 2. Type 2 virtual machines are more common today. They're what you get when a guest VM runs like an application on top of an existing OS. (This is VMware Workstation, Fusion, or Microsoft Virtual PC.)

Type 1 client-based virtual machines are also known as "bare metal" environments because the actual hypervisor is the local OS. So you have the hypervisor installed first, and then every desktop OS (Windows, Linux, etc.) runs as a guest VM inside that base-level hypervisor.

Many people in the industry—including those making and selling VDI products—thought that the major use case for client hypervisors was going to be to support something called offline VDI. The idea was that if we're converting all our desktops to run in VMs in our data centers, why not make it so that we can sort of sling the desktop VMs back and forth between laptops and data center servers. That way users can take their machines with them on their laptops when they need to travel, but they can still get the benefits of VDI when they're around an Internet connection.

What happened to offline VDI?

The concept of offline VDI seems cool when you first hear about it, but seeing as it was first discussed in the 2008-2009 time frame and it's now 2012, you can imagine that offline VDI didn't really catch on.

There were a few reasons for this. First, there was a holy war about the merits of Type 1 versus Type 2 hypervisors. For servers, it was easy—Type 1 was better. But for laptops and desktops, we started to see products emerge in both camps.

HOLY WAR

```
     XenClient              VMware Fusion
                             Workstation
       NxTop
                                Parallels
  Virtual Bridges
     VERDE LEAF
                             Virtual PC
    MokaFive
   Bare Metal
                             VirtualBox
  VMware CVP (x)

  Neocleus(x)               Win 7 XP Mode
```

The items with (x) shined dimly, for a very short time

Most people in the industry (ourselves included) believed that Type 1 client hypervisors would ultimately win out. What we hadn't really considered was that a Type 1 hypervisor running on a laptop is really hard to build! In our heads, we had oversimplified it, thinking it was just like putting ESX on a laptop.

In reality, ESX runs on servers. Server hardware is based on tightly controlled high-end components. The number of combinations of all those different components is large, but manageable when it comes to software development. Now consider the number of combinations of laptop hardware. Imagine the components in your laptop that you're not likely to find on the server. There's the fingerprint reader, WiFi, card reader, sound card, high-end graphics card with GPU, keyboard backlight sensor, battery and power management chips, and that little switch that tells the OS that you've closed the lid. Do you know what happens when you install ESX on a laptop and close the lid? Nothing.

Client hypervisors have to support all of those things on top of the processors, chipsets, network cards, and disk controllers that hypervisors need to support on the server side. Then consider that there are more variations between models, manufacturers, and quality on the client side, and you can see why it's taken so long.

As if that's not enough, when you're talking about a client hypervisor, all these various VMs and their management have to be drop-dead simple (or better yet, invisible) to the end users. You can't tell a user to recompile a driver from the Linux source to get their sound card to work. Users don't want to know that there's anything the slightest bit different going on, because if they found out, they'd blame everything on that one change.

Type 2 hypervisors, on the other hand, don't have nearly as many troubles, since they can rely on the host OS to take care of supporting all those devices. So Type 2 hypervisors (and their VMs) can run just about anywhere.

The downside to Type 2 is they're sort of at the mercy of the host OS. Performance of the VMs isn't as great because the Type 2 hypervisor has the same level of access to the host system as Angry Birds.

In the meantime, the whole industry was starting to realize that the whole concept of offline VDI didn't really make sense. First, we realized how complex the solution would have to be to enable synchronization of block- and file-level data between the client hypervisor and the server hypervisor. It would be hard enough to do that in real time with a continuous Internet connection, but imagine how much data would have to sync if the client were offline for a day or two. Now consider how much of that data isn't important and what it would take to sift out the relevant data on the fly and you can see that not only is offline VDI really complex, but it's not practical, either.

The other problem with offline VDI is that the whole reason companies use VDI in the first place is because they have a security concern or they want to allow their users to work from anywhere. If that's why you're using VDI, then offline VDI simply isn't an option for you because if you could use offline VDI, then why are you using VDI in the first place?

As an interesting footnote to the offline VDI battle, client hypervisors are actually making strides in the desktop industry now, and in fact, we like them quite a bit. The important takeaway is that offline VDI and client-based virtual machines (whether Type 1 or Type 2) are not really the same thing.

The new use cases for client-based VMs

The lack of offline VDI coupled with the ever-maturing client VM technology forced us to re-evaluate whether we can use client-based VMs in our organizations.

Type 1 solutions give the hypervisor direct hardware access, so as we mentioned before, it's possible to get pretty close to native performance from VMs running on them. Type 1 hypervisors also provide good security—there's no host OS to manage and multiple VMs can run at the same time with different amounts of security. In certain scenarios, Type 1 VMs can be easier to manage—in many cases, you can run the same VM with the same drivers on two different kinds of hardware.

On the downside, since Type 1 hypervisors replace the host OS with a stand-alone hypervisor, the installation is what we call "destructive" (meaning the hard drive has to be wiped to install a Type 1 hypervisor).

Type 2 solutions benefit from a normal user interface because they run right on top of Windows, Mac, or Linux, and they're easy to get up and running. Most companies like them because they're non-destructive. Installing a Type 2 hypervisor onto an existing laptop is no different than installing any standard application. This is great for scenarios where you want to deploy a VM to a user but you don't want to destroy or take over their drive. (This is perfect for contractors, users with personal laptops, etc.)

The downside to Type 2 hypervisors is that it's usually painfully obvious to the user that some sort of virtualization is going on. They have their full native desktop and then a second smaller desktop in a Window. Even if the user chooses to hide the background from the second desktop, it can be confusing, since some applications run on the host while others run in a VM. Finally, since Type 2 environments run the VM on top of a normal OS, it's possible for the host OS to capture data and activities from the guest. (What if a key logger or screen scraper was installed into the host without the user's knowledge?)

The bottom line about client-based virtual machines, whether Type 1 or Type 2, is that they're both environments where you can combine some of the advantages of managing VMs instead of desktops with the advantages of local computing. (They work offline, peripherals are supported, users can have graphically intense applications, and a user plugging in a USB drive won't take down the network.) In other words, client-based virtual machines are pretty much the exact opposite of data center-based virtual machines.

There are some not-so-good use cases

Before you get too excited about the prospects of client-based virtual machines, we want to be clear that we don't believe they're right for every use case. For example, Windows 7 and 8 have something called Windows XP Mode, which is Microsoft's attempt to help the transition away from Windows XP while still letting you run applications that aren't compatible with the latest versions of Windows. XP Mode works by using Microsoft Virtual PC (a Type 2 hypervisor that is almost never in the discussion) to actually run a Windows XP virtual machine on top of the Windows 7 or 8. This means that Microsoft's solution for XP desktop applications that aren't compatible with Windows 7 is to keep running them in XP.

The problem with this is that XP Mode is an unmanaged app, left to the user to maintain out of the box. Imagine if you used this on all the PCs in a 2,000-seat organization. You'd migrate from 2,000 Windows XP machines to 2,000 Windows 7 machines. Then you'd also create 2,000 new Windows XP virtual machines for a grand total of 4,000 Windows desktops to support. Congratulations, you've just doubled the number of desktops you have to manage! (Really you just added 2,000 Windows 7 desktops to your environment without taking anything away.)

OS Streaming

Have you ever heard of OS streaming? The general concept is that you take the hard disk out of a desktop computer and reconfigure its firmware so it boots from the network. Then during the boot process, it mounts a disk image from across the network instead of using a local disk. The idea is you get the security and benefits of central disk image management, but with Windows running at full speed on the individual computers.

OS streaming was initially popular in scenarios with a lot of desktop computers that all needed the same image that had to be changed or reset often. A great example was school labs. All the desktops could be powered on at once to access one disk image (with one set of apps), and then a simple reboot could enable them to access a different disk image with different apps. (This is why OS streaming was better than reimaging the desktops with something like Ghost—OS streaming was instant, whereas Ghost would take hours to reimage a machine.)

OS streaming sort of toiled in anonymity for years, mainly seen as part of the PC life-cycle management market. But when desktop virtualization became more popular a few years ago, OS streaming got some new respect.

First, the traditional model of OS streaming we just outlined definitely counts as a form of desktop virtualization. You have a bunch of physical desktops with no images in one location and a central image in another, and with a few clicks in an admin console you can assign any image to any computer.

More interestingly, many of the various forms of desktop virtualization involve running Windows in a VM (either in the data center via VDI or as a client-based VM as we described previously). All of those VMs boot from disk image files (usually VHD or VMDK), and we need some way to get those images from wherever they're stored to wherever they're executed. While we *could* copy the entire huge disk image file to the client or VM host ahead of time, that would be slow and isn't something we can do on demand. But if there were a way for the VM to boot and just connect to an image that's somewhere else... Hey! OS streaming suddenly is cool for desktop virtualization.

Now there are several dedicated OS streaming products, like Citrix Provisioning Server (part of XenDesktop) and Wyse Streaming Manager. Dell and Lenovo also have offerings, and many of the storage vendors (and some WAN acceleration vendors) are coming out with things like "diskless VDI," which allows any VDI desktop to boot to any disk image without a SAN. So whether you're thinking about this for a virtual machine or a physical desktop, OS streaming lets a machine boot in one location while the image lives in another—something you should absolutely consider as you're putting together your desktop strategy.

Traditional Desktops

You're probably wondering why we include traditional desktops as a type of desktop virtualization. As you'll see throughout the rest of this book, we're huge fans of thinking about desktops as a whole (rather than focusing on traditional desktops versus virtual desktops).

This is a good thing for most of us considering that traditional desktops make up the vast majority of corporate desktops in the world. We have years of experience dealing with them, and we're pretty familiar with their overall life cycle:

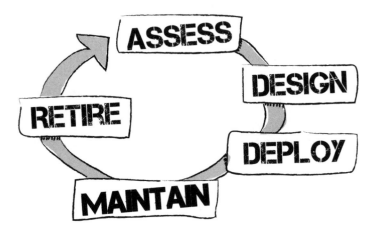

While there are many different reasons for virtualizing desktops, the reality is that every virtual desktop is essentially replacing an existing traditional desktop. The conversations about what to virtualize are really about which of your existing physical desktops to virtualize. But since it's unlikely that you'll virtualize all of them, you'll be left with a bunch of physical desktops that you'll still have to deal with. Some people view this as a failure or being stuck in the old way of doing things. Other people just shrug it off and keep doing what they've been doing. Our view is that if the traditional desktops have been meeting your needs, why change?

If you're being pushed into desktop virtualization by a drive to re-evaluate everything you're doing with desktops, you can also take this opportunity to re-evaluate how you manage your physical desktop, too. So even though you might think these physical ones "failed" because you can't virtualize them, they can probably still benefit from many of the things you're putting in place for your virtual desktop environment.

For example, if you're virtualizing applications or creating a corporate app store for your virtual desktops, why not deliver those same virtual apps to your physical desktops? If you're implementing some kind of user personality or data syncing tool for your virtual desktops, extend that to your physical desktops.

All These Choices Make Things Complex!

Your main takeaway from this chapter should be that there are many ways to deliver Windows desktops to users. In the old days, the only option was to install Windows locally on each desktop. Then we had RDSH. Then VDI. Then client-based VMs. Then streaming. Next we'll have Windows from outer space or something. Our point is that there are a lot of ways to get Windows to your users. None is better or worse than the other, as each delivery method is appropriate for different scenarios.

The only downside to all this choice is that, well, we have a choice now! In the old days, it was simple to design our Windows strategy because there was only one option. But now—yikes! How do you pick which delivery technology you're going to use? The short answer is that you're going to have to mix and match these various technologies in your environment.

When we give presentations about this topic, we use a slide that illustrates how all the various desktop technologies build upon one another. We show that you might start with 500 traditional desktops, which we represent as blue squares. Then we add 100 RDSH desktops (green squares), 50 VDI desktops (red), 100 client-based virtual machines (purple), and finally a few dozen OS streamed desktops (yellow):

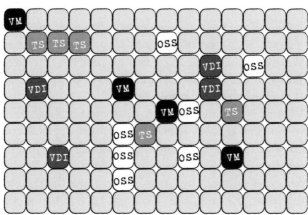

(If you're reading the printed version of this book, you'll have to use your imagination for the color here.)

Whenever we present our story in public, there are usually people in the audience who don't like it. They say, "Hey! I thought desktop virtualization was supposed to simplify my life. But what you're showing is far more complex than what I'm doing now! Are you advocating this rainbow of complexity?"

Our response to this is, "Well...yes!" Yes, this is a complex solution, and yes, having five different ways of delivering the Windows desktop is more complex than having one. So we completely agree that this rainbow of colored boxes is more complex than if it were just one color.

But let's be clear on one thing: All these various desktop delivery methods are not the cause of the complexity. They are the *effect*.

As desktop architects, we're forced to use all these different desktop delivery methods because the world of business is changing. After all, it's the business that wants users to be able to access their desktops via their iPads from the golf course. They're the ones who want to enable thousands of users to work from home as easily as they can from the office. They're the ones who want to provide tens of thousands of university students with a consistent desktop environment that they can access from their Mac laptops, campus labs, or the coffee shop.

So yes, this stuff is complex. But that's the world's fault, not ours. If our business requirements today were the same as they were in 1995, then we could get away with only having physical desktops and a single way of working for about one-tenth the price of what we're trying to do now. But our business requirements have changed. This rainbow of complexity is our only chance to support the business's crazy requirements.

All of these various desktop delivery options lead to one inevitable question: How do you decide which type of desktop virtualization you should use for which users? Fortunately, that's pretty much what the rest of this book covers. The next chapter begins with the first step, which is that in order to pick the right kind of desktop delivery for your users, you first have to figure out what your goals are. Let's dig in!

Chapter 6

What Are You Trying to Solve?

IT WOULD BE ACCURATE TO SAY that the chapters in this book can be roughly grouped into three parts. The first covers the promise of VDI and desktop virtualization, while the second looks at the reality of the technologies. This chapter begins the third part of the book, which is focused on the specific actions you can take in your own environment.

Since we have backgrounds as consultants (or two of us do— one of us was a music major), we know that the first step to a successful consulting project is to figure out what your goals are. So that's what this chapter is about: What are your goals for VDI and desktop virtualization? What problem are you trying to solve?

We've spent the past half-dozen chapters or so digging into the technologies that make up desktop virtualization and looking at the pros and cons of each. So now, instead of focusing on specific scenarios each technology can solve, we're going to elevate the thinking a bit and try to figure out, philosophically speaking, why companies choose to use desktop virtualization.

In your environment, what exactly are you trying to do?

- Do you want to save costs?
- Do you want the help desk phone to stop ringing?
- Do you want to allow your users to work from anywhere?
- Do you want your users to be able to work from iPads or other tablets?

- Do you want your users to be able to use Macs, or to bring their own computers into your environment?

- Do you want your users to be able to use whatever smart phone they want while still being able to hook into your corporate apps?

- Do you want your company to be able to attract a younger generation of workers who won't accept locked-down, Windows-based laptops made out of plastic?

- Do you want your users to be able to use all the latest web, SaaS, and consumer apps, while still being able to securely integrate with your corporate apps?

- Do you need to increase the security of your desktops and applications?

- Do you want to prevent a laptop hard drive crash from causing user data loss?

- Do you want to get out of the business of managing end-user computing hardware?

We could go on and probably fill a hundred pages with potential ideas for things you can do with desktop virtualization. The point is not to give you a list to pick from, but rather it's to get you thinking about what you're trying to accomplish. From there you can decide which type (if any) of desktop virtualization is right for you and what your specific implementation goals should be.

Even though we're starting to sound like a broken record on this, we'll say it again: Desktop virtualization is not right for every desktop or every company. It makes sense in some cases, but there are plenty of scenarios where no desktop virtualization is needed.

Why Companies Choose to Virtualize Their Desktops

We already talked about the specific advantages of the various types of desktop virtualization. VDI and RDSH provide easier management, access from anywhere, consistent performance, and the potential for great security; client VMs give us a way to manage the Windows instance separately from the hardware, etc. But all of those advantages are very specific and tactical. They don't really address the business-based philosophical reasons that companies choose to use desktop virtualization.

So let's take a look at some of the most common reasons IT admins list when asked why they're using desktop virtualization. This is based on our experience talking to people, comments on blogs, polls via Twitter, and just being out in the world. We feel this is a good representation of what people are actually doing.

Enable users to work from anywhere

Perhaps the greatest benefit of the data center-based Windows desktop (including desktops delivered via VDI or RDSH) is that it enables users to access their full work desktop from anyway with no advanced planning. A user can walk up to just about any Internet-connected device on the planet and within 100 keystrokes or so be using his or her own corporate desktop complete with their apps, data, settings, and everything.

From the perspective of IT, this is great because the user gets the same experience wherever they are. All their apps are there. All their data is there. They can do whatever they need to, and they don't have to mess around with VPNs and drive mapping and syncing and client scans and everything else that's associated with connecting a laptop to a remote environment. And of course we can't overemphasize the beauty of not having to plan in advance. The user doesn't have to check anything out. The user doesn't even have to remember to bring a laptop with them.

Many companies use this primarily for teleworkers (people working from home). A central desktop that's served to the users via VDI or RDSH is a great way to ensure that the users get a consistent experience from whatever device they happen to be using.

Some companies also choose to simply use the data center-based desktop as an auxiliary desktop. In those cases, the users might still have a standard physical desktop or laptop that they use as their primary device, but they also have the ability to log in from anywhere to a secondary desktop when they need to. This is great for the unexpected snow day or G8 protest, as the alternate desktop is available immediately, with no need to set anything up ahead of time.

In fact, if you provide an auxiliary desktop from a data center, you don't necessarily have to provide the same 100% full desktop experience for the user as their everyday desktop. Maybe your users use corporate laptops with all their apps installed locally as their primary devices, but then as a backup option they can access an RDSH session with just the basic apps installed. Sure, they can't do everything, but they can log in, access the corporate files and their documents, and use Office and email—certainly enough to get a decent amount of work done.

The important thing is that the people who are currently using VDI and RDSH to enable their users to work from anywhere are *not*, generally speaking, forcing this upon all their users all the time. It's all just part of the trade-off.

Allow users to use whatever devices they want

The second most popular reason people say they use desktop virtualization is that it lets their users use whatever devices they want. This is great because IT doesn't have to tell users, "No, you can't use that," which means users are happier. It also means that IT has less to worry about. Your IT staff doesn't have to follow what all the latest devices are and keep track of all the features. If a user wants to bring in some random device that you've never heard of, chances are there's a client for it that can connect into your remote desktop environment. Heck, your users can bring in a new device every week for all you care, because with desktop virtualization, it's not your problem!

Keep in mind that letting your users use whatever devices they want does not automatically mean you have to put your corporate desktop in the data center and deliver it via VDI or RDSH. If you let users pick whatever laptop they want, you can still have your corporate desktop running locally on the laptop—just use a client-based desktop virtualization option to give it to them in the form of a VM. (This works regardless of whether your users choose Windows, Mac, or Linux laptops.) You can have your centrally managed, locally executed, domain-joined, completely locked-down corporate VM on their laptop where the users can't do anything. Then that runs on top of the host OS where the user has full control. So you have all the benefits of local computing—offline use, great peripheral access, and the ability to run 3-D, graphically intense apps, all while maintaining the ultimate lockdown and control.

By the way, notice that we didn't specifically call this section BYO (Bring Your Own). While a lot of companies are using desktop virtualization technologies to enable BYOC (Bring Your Own Computer) programs, you can use desktop virtualization to let users work from any device regardless of whether the corporation owns the device or the users own it. In fact, there are a lot of companies that don't want to do BYOC but that still give their users locked-down corporate desktops in VMs just to make the users happy and the IT staff's lives easier.

Allow users to do and install whatever they want

Another advantage of desktop virtualization that's related to letting users use whatever device they want is that you can also let users install whatever apps they want (and generally "do" whatever they want) while you still maintain control of your corporate image.

Remember toward the beginning of the book we talked about how most users have admin rights and the ability to install or do whatever they want on their laptops and how taking that away from them with desktop virtualization was a bad idea. (Well, taking it away is hard to do, and a lot of people try to do it at the same time that they implement desktop virtualization, which leads to desktop virtualization getting blamed for upsetting all the users.)

But if you use desktop virtualization to provide the corporate desktop and apps and then let users do whatever they want on their devices, you just might be able to bargain with them. It might be possible to take away their admin rights on the corporate desktop in exchange for the user being able to install Angry Birds and Dropbox on their laptops or tablets.

Deliver Windows applications to non-Windows tablets

While it's somewhat related to letting the users use whatever devices they want, tablets are a big enough deal now that they're worth discussing separately. A lot of companies (and we mean a lot) simply use the VDI and RDSH forms of desktop virtualization as a way to deliver Windows desktops and apps to touch-based, non-Windows tablets. (Today, that's mainly iPads and Android tablets, though in the future it will also include Windows 8 on ARM tablets, since those won't be able to natively run non-Metro apps.)

For the record, we don't believe for one second that this is a good user experience, but hey, if the users want to access corporate Windows desktop applications from their iPads, who are we to say no? (Especially because it's usually the doctors, lawyers, and execs who are the ones who want to do this.)

The good news is that these days, most apps have specific touch-based iOS or Android versions available. For example, users with iPads don't connect to VDI to run Outlook—they use the built-in iPad mail app. The same is true for Dropbox, Salesforce, analytics data visualizers, Safari, WebEx, etc. There are great iPad apps for all of these. But if the user needs that obscure Windows-based app on their iPad, VDI or RDSH can do it!

Security at any cost

Many people using VDI and RDSH today do so simply because they need the high security that exists only when the entire desktop is running in the data center. This means that there's nothing running, stored, or cached on the endpoint, which is great for a few reasons.

For companies that are concerned about intellectual property, it means they can outsource work without worrying that the people they're outsourcing it to are going to copy all their files or steal all their code.

For organizations that need to think about physical device theft, these data center-based desktops are great because if anyone steals a client device, there's nothing on it. And if that client device is a thin client, it doesn't do anything on its own anyway and hopefully won't be stolen in the first place.

For companies that have to worry about regulation and compliance issues, keeping everything in the data center means they don't have to worry about an employee's laptop getting stolen, leading to an embarrassing publicity moment and the need to purchase two years of a credit monitoring service for two million of their best customers.

What Do All These Use Cases Have in Common?

These examples are the ones that come up again and again when we ask people to tell us their Number 1 reason for using desktop virtualization. As we said earlier, they're certainly not the only reasons to use desktop virtualization, but they're the most common.

Now that you've read through that list, what do you notice about these reasons? What do they all have in common? We think three things:

They're all tactical and specific

In every example of companies that are successful with desktop virtualization, we see that they have specific and achievable goals. They're not doing desktop virtualization just because virtualization is cool or just because they virtualized their servers. They're not hopping on any trend. Instead, they each have a specific goal they're trying to meet.

Also notice that none of the people who are successful with desktop virtualization try to apply it to 100% of their users, apps, devices, or use cases. They'll use RDSH for the apps they need to run in the data center. They'll use VDI for the specific users where they're worried about security. They'll only put client VMs on certain machines where it makes sense. They're not just trying to blindly roll out desktop virtualization and suck up everyone and everything.

They all apply to more than one style of desktop virtualization

Second, notice that many of these goals can be achieved by more than one type of desktop virtualization. If you want to let your users have Macs, you can deliver a Windows desktop to them via VDI, RDSH, or a client-based virtual machine. None of these solutions are VDI-only or client VM-only solutions, and the companies that are successful know they have to use the right technology and the right delivery mechanism for the right scenario.

They all still involve Windows

Finally, notice that all of these use cases for desktop virtualization still involve Windows. No one is using desktop virtualization to get away from Windows or to get out of managing Windows. They're using desktop virtualization for the flexibility, security, and resilience—of Windows.

Traditional Desktops Aren't Actually That Bad

If you look at the commonalities of why people choose to use desktop virtualization, you see that they're not trying to replace Windows and they're not trying to virtualize 100% of their desktops. This means that even in the companies that have chosen to implement desktop virtualization, there are still a lot of traditional, physical Windows-based desktop and laptops in their environment.

Hopefully by now you realize this is okay. Really, that's the point we've spent half the book trying to make. It's like parents with two kids—they have the capacity to love them both equally. We love both desktop virtualization and traditional non-virtual Windows desktops equally.

It makes sense and helps explain why traditional Windows desktops and laptops have been around for 20-plus years. Ironically, it took the shortfalls of desktop virtualization to realize that what we had right in front of us—the traditional physical desktop—wasn't actually that bad. We basically know how to manage them, we know that they can run any application locally and don't need an Internet connection to function, and we know what we're getting into. Users know how to use them, how to install and remove applications, and generally how to get around.

It's fair to say that the future of desktop virtualization involves traditional Windows desktops. (Or maybe we should say that the future of the Windows desktop involves virtualization?) Either way, we know that desktop virtualization and Windows desktops are very closely related. So let's continue our journey toward the future desktop by trying to figure out what exactly a desktop is.

Chapter 7

Understanding Windows

BACK IN CHAPTER 5, WE EXPLORED several different technologies (VDI, RDSH, client VMs, etc.) that all need to be considered as you put together your desktop strategy. Then in the last chapter, we looked at what problems you can realistically hope to solve with desktop virtualization. Both chapters touched on an important fact—desktop virtualization, at least in 2012, is about delivering Microsoft Windows to your users.

Even though we have to deal with the complexity of multiple technologies and multiple goals, we still have to try to find ways to simplify it. The way we do that is to find elements that are the same across all the different forms of delivery. Doing that is almost like removing elements from mathematical formulas that cancel each other out on opposite sides of the equation.

In fact, this is what many people claim the core promise of desktop virtualization to be, although if you're reading this book in order, you know that we pretty much tore that apart in Chapter 4. But that doesn't mean we don't want to simplify, thus we need to look for commonalities across all these different desktop delivery scenarios.

Do you know what the biggest commonality is? It's practically staring us in the face: the Microsoft Windows operating system! VDI, RDSH, client-based virtual machines, streamed disk images—every one of these involves a desktop running Windows. So if you can get your Windows environment under control, the actual delivery mechanism you use is immaterial.

Why Are We Still Dealing with Windows?

Hundreds of books have been written about Microsoft and their Windows OS, and loads of scholars have argued about why Microsoft came to prominence and how we found ourselves in this situation. So we're not going to go into that history here. Instead, we'll just point out a few important facts that are shaping the desktop virtualization landscape today:

- We live in a Windows world.
- Windows desktop applications are not going anywhere anytime soon.
- If you have Windows desktop applications, you have to deal with the Windows OS.

Let's dig into each of these in a bit more detail.

Reality No. 1: We live in a Windows world

Like it or not, we're living in a world where the majority of current corporate and enterprise applications are Windows-based.

Nearly everyone agrees that Microsoft's dominance of the IT world will end at some point. In fact, some studies have shown that as of 2011, the majority of new applications deployed in the enterprise were not Windows-based.

While that study is likely true, it's only talking about new applications. But just because a lot of new apps are non-Windows native applications, there are still a lot of existing Windows-based apps. This leads us to our second reality about Windows.

Reality No. 2: Windows applications are not going anywhere anytime soon

Corporations have invested millions upon millions of dollars in their enterprise apps—both software they've purchased and implemented and apps they've written themselves. And as every

IT veteran knows now, you can't just wave a magic wand and move your enterprise from one app to another.

Sure, maybe the majority of new apps that enterprises are choosing today are non-Windows apps. That's awesome! But we're going to be dealing with those preexisting Windows apps for years—if not decades—to come.

If you don't believe this, think about mainframes and main-frame apps. When were those considered obsolete? Twenty years ago? Thirty? Yet NASA just decommissioned their last mainframe in 2012, and as of this writing, when you check in to a United Airlines flight, that agent is using United's custom-built SHARES software, which is mainframe-driven. (Peek your head over the counter. You'll see a Windows 7 desktop—with terminal emu-lation software connecting back to a green-screen app. And it's 2012!)

Microsoft Windows apps will follow the same course. Year after year, organizations will slowly move away from their Micro-soft desktop apps. They'll slowly move to HTML5 or web-based or iOS or whatever clients. But there will be some (if only residual) Windows apps around for a long, long time. This brings us to our third reality about Windows apps.

Reality No. 3: Windows apps require a Windows OS

Imagine that as the number of traditional Windows apps a company uses gets smaller and smaller, the company will eventu-ally get to the point where they have only a few straggling Win-dows apps left. Yay! Unfortunately, if you have even one Windows app anywhere in your environment, that means you need to have a Windows OS somewhere. And having a Windows OS means that you have to deal with a Windows user account and a Windows user profile and DLLs and application settings and the registry and domain computer properties and licensing and...well, you get the point.

So while there's a good chance that you might ultimately be able to get out of the "end-user device management" game at some point, there's an equally good chance that someone at your company is going to be dealing with Windows for the next ten or twenty years.

The bottom line is that no matter how you slice it, if your job involves delivering apps to users, you're going to need to deal with Windows, like it or not!

Why Is Windows So Difficult?

We'll be first in line to curse at Microsoft for holding back our industry. (Who's the jerk in Redmond who's not allowing Windows desktop SPLA licenses?) But we'll also give credit where credit is due, and Microsoft deserves a lot for building, promoting, and cultivating the entire Windows ecosystem, which is now greater than 1 billion computers. (That's not an exaggeration. There are over 1 billion computers in the world running Windows!)

If you think back to the time when Windows was initially architected, that was a world where one user equaled one computer, which equaled one copy of the Windows OS. And Microsoft's main goal then was to provide a way for all the various applications to be integrated together and for all the users' settings and data to be used by all the applications. Back then, Microsoft didn't have the tight control on the world that they do now, so one of the ways they encouraged developers to write for the Windows platform was to essentially allow them to do whatever they wanted. Need the user to have admin rights for your app to work? No problem! Need to hard-code your app to store critical files in the root of the C: drive? Sure thing! Want your app to access the hardware directly and bypass the Windows APIs? Bring it on!

You can imagine how 20-plus years of this laissez faire approach to regulating the Windows environment has resulted in the current state of the Windows application market with literally hundreds of thousands of apps, some that work well, some that don't, some that conflict with each other, some that install no problem. And consider that many of these apps were written with the idea that one copy of the application would be installed onto one physical machine, which was to be used by the same single user day after day. After thinking about it, you sort of wonder how even the simplest aspects of this Windows desktop virtualization concept are possible at all?

This isn't the book to get into all the gory details about why it's tough to manage Windows, but in the context of desktop virtualization, there are a few key themes that we see again and again:

First, when it comes to applications, you can't just copy a few files onto the computer to install an app. Instead, you have to go through the app's installation routine, which often does many things, like put files into the Program Files folder, install device drivers, install Windows services, add or update DLLs, make additions to both the system registry and the user registry, copy files to the user's home drive, set up the default configuration for the user, enable file protection to "self-heal" if anything goes missing, register itself with the hardware or software update services, etc.

We also have problems with applications conflicting with each other. Sometimes you have two apps that want to use the same piece of hardware, or different versions of the same DLL, or the same files or service names.

Both of these things mean that when it comes to apps, (1) you can't just "copy" the files—you have to install the apps, and (2) you have to know what other apps are already installed on that computer before you can know whether or not your app will even work after you install it! This is exacerbated by the fact that many companies allow their users to have administrative rights in their Windows desktops, which means the users can install software on their own. In this environment, it's possible that a needed corporate app might not work because it conflicts with some piece-of-garbage app that the user has installed!

In addition to these application complexities, another big problem with Windows is that the whole concept of the Windows user profile doesn't make sense in today's modern times. The Windows user profile is the collection of user settings that includes things like the wallpaper, system fonts, and menu colors, but also the user's Start Menu, Internet favorites, and My Documents. The main problems with user profiles are (1) they don't store everything the user does or changes—only the subset of changes that are saved in a special folder or the user-specific area of the registry, and (2) there's no good central way to handle user profiles if the user logs onto more than one Windows desktop at the same time. (Of course this wasn't a problem when Windows was designed in the 1990s, but now that it's possible for users to have one or two virtual desktops, plus a local laptop and a few applications they remotely connect to on RDSH servers, it's a huge problem today!)

In recent years, some companies have tried to "solve" the Windows problem by going to web apps. Sure, they know that they can't move to 100% web apps, but they figure the more web apps they use, the fewer Windows apps they need, and every little bit helps, right?

While you might think that's true at first, it seems like a lot of corporate web-based applications have very specific web browser requirements—for example, they need a certain browser with a certain version of Java with a specific plug-in—and of course different web apps have different requirements. Multiply the different requirements needed for each app, and after time it becomes impossible to even have a single browser configuration that works for all these things!

And then of course there's the constant, never-ending barrage of Windows OS software updates, security updates, antivirus and anti-spyware updates—the list goes on and on! And sometimes these updates break certain apps, so now you've got to test all this stuff, too!

We could go on and on, but the bottom line is this: Every one of these complexities applies to Windows itself, which means that everything listed here is something you have to deal with regardless of whether you use VDI or client-based VMs or RDSH or streamed local disks or good old-fashioned traditional physical desktops. And since having even one Windows app means that you have to deal with all these complexities, you're going to be dealing with these things for decades to come.

Remember, desktop virtualization *does not fix this!* Desktop virtualization is simply a way to deliver desktops and apps to users. Desktop virtualization is just a new form of the desktop, just like the laptop was a new form of the desktop. But desktop virtualization is not a magic wand that will make these Windows complexities go away—just like having multiple users share the same disk image doesn't make these problems go away. (And honestly, if sharing the same image did make the problems go away, all 500 million corporate desktops in the world would have been using Symantec Ghost since 1994!)

Bonus Tip: If You Want To Really Learn Windows, Read the Resource Kit

One final thought for this chapter: If you want to become an expert at desktop virtualization, the best thing you can do is to read the Windows 7 Resource Kit published by Microsoft Press. It's about 1,700 pages, but if you read this cover-to-cover, we guarantee you'll be a better desktop virtualization expert than 99% of IT pros who attempt to understand desktop virtualization! (Heck, just knowing that desktop virtualization is more about Windows 7 desktops and less about virtualization will put you ahead of about 80% of the pack.)

Seriously, finish this book and then read the Resource Kit, and you'll be unstoppable!

Chapter 8

What Is a Desktop?

$\mathbf{T}$HIS ENTIRE BOOK IS ABOUT DESKTOP VIRTUALIZATION and the future of the Windows desktop. But before we explore this further, we need to take a step back and define what exactly a desktop is.

For the past twenty years, when people heard the word "desktop," they thought of a physical computer with a keyboard and mouse that ran Microsoft Windows. More recently, people have started to think of the desktop as a VM that runs Windows. But we'd like to take this a step further.

The Desktop Is More Than a Computer Running Windows

The main reason people think "Windows" when they think about the desktop is because, for all intents and purposes, Windows and the desktop have always been the same thing. But if you look at what Windows actually does, you see it performs many different—and somewhat unrelated—functions. For example, the Windows desktop is:

- The literal operating system instance that interacts with the hardware.
- The user interface that the user sees—including the wallpaper, Start Menu, and app icons.

- A runtime environment that allows Win32 applications to execute and interact with each other.
- A container of configuration settings.
- A container for security, including the ability for the user to launch processes and connect to resources in their context.
- The boundary that surrounds a user's apps, settings, and data.

Looking at it like this, we see that Windows does a lot! But for the past twenty years, we've casually lumped all of these different items into the catchall called the "Windows desktop." We did this out of necessity because there was no way to separate out any of the individual pieces. Windows, as we said, was a monolithic brick.

You could even say that most desktop virtualization efforts so far have been about virtualizing this monolithic brick of a desktop. Whether we put that brick on a server (VDI), on a laptop (client-based VM), or deliver it to an iPad (via VDI), we're not really changing anything about the way that Windows works—we're just finding new ways to make sure users can access their monolithic brick. (Some have used the analogy that it's like going from a typewriter to an electric typewriter. Sure, it's fancy, but it's not Microsoft Word.)

Looking ahead, however, it's easy to see that there's no reason that all six of the desktop elements listed above can't be broken up and delivered independently. They can be pulled apart, transformed, and reassembled into some other form. That would give us something with all the characteristics of what we're calling a desktop, but it sure wouldn't look like one.

For example, is an iPad a desktop? It has an OS to interact with the hardware. It has a user interface that lets the user launch applications and configure system settings, and it lets admins apply centralized configuration and security settings. So by our definition, it seems like the iPad certainly is a desktop, right?

What, you don't agree? Why not? Because it doesn't run Windows apps? Because it doesn't have real multitasking? Because it doesn't have a built-in keyboard? None of those requirements are on our list, and besides, there are plenty of desktops that don't run Windows and plenty of slate PCs that run Windows but don't have a physical keyboard. And of course there will be a lot of Windows 8 ARM-based tablets without keyboards that only run Metro-style apps from the Windows Store. Are those desktops?

Can you see the complexity of fixating on a definition here? On the one hand, it's easy to say, "Who cares? So what if we can't define exactly what a desktop is?" But on the other hand, this book is about desktop virtualization and the future of desktops. So how can we know how to virtualize these things and what the future looks like if we can't even define the basic term?

It's fascinating that we haven't had to deal with the "what is a desktop" conversation in the world of IT because the "desktop" hasn't changed in twenty years. It's only now that we have tablets with their own apps, phones with their own apps, Mac laptops with their own apps, and tons of web apps that we're actually taking a step back and trying to figure out what we're doing.

A Desktop Without a Desktop?

Our list of six characteristics of a desktop notwithstanding, we believe that in today's world, a desktop is defined as a collection of a user's applications, settings, and data. This desktop is a philosophical concept—not a physical device. It has to be able to access and run applications that may be platform-dependent local apps or platform-agnostic web apps.

In our world, the desktop itself is nothing more than the container (or glue) that holds everything else together. So if a user has an iPad with a lot of applications and data and settings and they can work from it—that's a desktop. The same is true for a laptop running Microsoft Windows. To us, it doesn't matter as long as the user has access to the apps, settings, and data.

What about the past twenty years in which the world has thought of the Microsoft Windows desktop as the desktop? Were they all wrong? Of course not. It's just that in the past, the only way to deliver, package, and integrate apps, settings, and data was by managing and delivering a Microsoft Windows OS. But in today's world, if we can deliver a user's apps, settings, and data to their iPad via a combination of iOS native and web apps, then that's certainly a desktop, too.

So moving forward, we'll separate out the apps and deliver them to whatever device the user has, meaning the user won't be locked to a specific device. We'll allow the user to maintain their settings and configuration no matter how they connect, and we'll ensure the user is able to access the needed data and files from anywhere. That will be our desktop.

Does This Mean the Traditional Desktop Is Dead?

Whenever we talk about how the future of the desktop is not about delivering Microsoft Windows desktops, people always ask us, "Is the PC dead?" or "Is the desktop dead?" (That fire is stoked by the constant drumbeat of Bay Area executives who claim, "We've entered the post-PC era.")

Our belief is that we have entered an era in which people can choose to use their smart phones or tablets in situations that would have previously required them to lug around a whole laptop. But that's not quite the same thing as saying, "The PC is dead."

We can say with great confidence that the delivery of the monolithic Windows desktop will be dead at some point. But that doesn't mean that no one will run Windows on their computers. It just means that we won't deliver the desktop as a single brick to the users. Instead, we'll deliver all the various components that will coalesce on whatever device the user happens to be using. But that device could end up being a Microsoft Windows desktop. (And it probably *will* end up being a Microsoft Windows desktop for years to come.)

The tablet's role in the supposed death of the PC

Let's face it: Users love tablets. Computer makers love to sell tablets. And Microsoft is embracing tablets and touch features like crazy for Windows 8. So tablets and touch-based computing are huge. But there's a lot of work that's hard to do on a tablet, since it doesn't have a real keyboard, a precision pointing device, or a lot of screen real estate. (Sure, you can carry a Bluetooth keyboard with you, but then why not just get an Ultrabook or MacBook Air?) The point is that for the foreseeable future—at least ten years—there will still be a need for devices with keyboards and mice. They might not run a copy of Windows that was dropped down in a monolithic brick form, but they'll have keyboards and mice and will be around for a long time.

This doesn't mean that we can trivialize tablets just because we don't think that users can do "real" work on them, because users sure love those things. (Oh, who are we kidding—we do too!) But in their own little way, tablets are contributing to the decline of the desktop.

First, tablets are a new device—a third device—that everyone will use. This really blew away the notion of the PC era in which everything you have is "on" a device. In the days when we only had smart phones, it was possible to sync our phone to our computer, but now with a third device, it's just too complex to sync device to device to device, so we just moved to syncing with and storing data in the cloud. And once we set that precedent, whether we have three devices or thirty devices doesn't really matter. This took the focus away from the monolithic desktop.

Second, users aren't trading in their PCs for tablets. There's no "convergence" here, or whatever B.S. the tablet vendors are calling it now. Sure, users might leave their laptops at home and only take an iPad on a trip with them, but in general, tablets are being purchased to augment PCs, not to replace them. That means that while people love to touch their tablets with multiple fingers at the same time, they still go back to a keyboard, mouse, and dual 24-inch screens when they're sitting down to get focused work done.

Third, the tablet ushered in the idea that end-user consumers are able to choose their own apps. Consumers expect those apps to be cheap (or free), and they expect them to be always up to date. Consumers also expect the OS to be updated and for that update to be free. (Remember the outcry when Apple tried to charge ten bucks to upgrade iOS on an iPod touch? People freaked out, even though charging for OS upgrades is totally normal in the PC world.)

Rumors of the PC's death have been greatly exaggerated

So everyone will use tablets, and PCs won't be used as much, since tablets will do in most cases. These are both true statements. But PCs aren't going anywhere anytime soon.

If you want to know how awesome a PC is (and again, remember that the term "PC" here means any traditional computer—laptop, desktop, Mac, Windows, etc.), just try using a tablet as your only device and see how well that works out for you.

Some people say, "Well, of course the tablet isn't usable now, but that's because a lot of our apps are not designed for touch. If they were, it would be fine, tablets would rule, and the PC would be dead." But we say "Balderdash!" to that. For the things people want to do that need keyboards, they don't need a version of the app that's made for touch—they need a device with a keyboard and mouse!

Other people claim the PC is dead because you can use desktop virtualization to deliver a remote-hosted VDI or RDSH session to a tablet. While this is great for emergencies, Windows desktop applications are intended to be used with a keyboard and mouse. Tablet lovers then claim that you can dock your tablet with a full-size screen, keyboard, and mouse, but if you do that, your tablet is nothing more than a thin client you always have with you. That's not the tablet winning at all—that's Windows with a keyboard and mouse winning!

Computing is all about choosing the right form factor for the right task. Sure, some of us don't have lots of different devices so we try to type on a touchscreen or we read books on our laptops.

But in general, we use the right device for the right task, and even in this world of tablets, phones, and cloud storage, a computing device with a keyboard and mouse—regardless of its OS—plays a big role.

So is the PC dead? Hardly. The idea of the Windows desktop as a monolithic chunk is starting to go away, but devices with keyboards and mice that run Windows will be around for a long time.

Chapter 9

How Do We Make Windows Do This?

L**ET'S REVIEW WHAT WE'VE COVERED SO FAR.** We've established that a desktop is more of a concept than a specific monolithic installation of Windows. We also discussed that Windows desktop applications are going to be around for a long time, even as IT departments focus less on Windows desktop management. We talked about how users are increasingly demanding access to their applications regardless of where they are and what type of device they're using. And finally, while the traditional desktop PC may be in its twilight years, devices with keyboards and mice will live on.

Given these truths, let's start figuring out how we can provide our services to support this new way of working. In this chapter, we're going to specifically focus on how we can shoehorn our traditional (yet very important) Windows desktop applications into this new paradigm. Then in the next chapter, we'll look at the impact of the "new age" (i.e., non-Windows apps), followed by a few chapters explaining how we tie it all together.

By the way, some have suggested that trying to fit traditional Windows desktop applications into this new device- and form factor-agnostic world is like trying to force a square peg in a round hole. The good news is that we couldn't agree more! The bad news is that even though we all think it's hard to fit a square peg in a round hole, we still have to somehow figure out how to do it. (After all, most of our critical apps today are square pegs, and our users only want to use devices with round holes.) So whether we have to shave it, pound it, bend it, or force it—one way or another we're going to have to figure out how to get that square-pegged Windows desktop application into the round hole of today's devices. (And as soon as we figure that out, users are going to want to put our square pegs into triangle holes. Then star-shaped holes. Then...)

Focus on the Applications

No IT department ever really wanted to focus on desktops. Even in our old-school 1990s desktop world, what did the desktop really ever do? Mainly it was just an OS and user interface for the device the user was staring at, and even then it was just a way for the user to use applications and access data. So even back then, IT departments only cared about the applications and data. It's just that we didn't have a way to separate out the applications and data from the desktop, so we were like, "Dang! I guess dealing with this Windows desktop B.S. is a necessary evil that we have to address in order to provide our users with access to our apps and data."

Our fantasy would be to just provide the applications and data without providing the desktop, which would be great because we could stop worrying about the end users' client devices. The way to do this is to figure out how you can provide Windows desktop applications as a service. (Some people also call this "service-oriented" application delivery.) We freely admit that this sounds like some lame thing that was made up by marketing consultants, but trust us—this approach is legit!

If you can reorient the way you deliver desktop applications so you're providing them as a service, you can separate yourself from the users' device management—you manage the application, they manage the device. This is exactly the way that most SaaS vendors work. Salesforce and Gmail don't worry about your client device—they just say, "You need a web browser. Point it to our site." Done!

Of course this service orientation is simple for new companies with new applications, because they designed everything to work this way from day one. Their apps are already written as web apps, and they're all ready to go. But we're talking about Windows desktop applications here, which unfortunately already exist in Windows desktop form. So while you might be running web apps exclusively twenty years from now, the immediate issue is to figure out how to convert the old-school Windows desktop applications into something that you can deliver as a service.

Does this mean we can avoid managing Windows now?

Remember one of the key points from earlier in this book was that implementing desktop virtualization does not relieve you of the need to manage Windows desktops. But here we're saying, "Hey! If you just deliver your Windows desktop applications as a service, then you don't have to worry about the end user's desktop!" So what gives?

What gives is that in converting your Windows desktop applications to be delivered as a service, it's true that you don't have to worry about managing Windows on your users' endpoints. But you do still have to worry about managing the Windows instance that supports the desktop applications that you're delivering, and that may include user accounts, user profiles, licenses, data, security policies, the registry, DLLs, etc. So even service-orienting your Windows desktop applications doesn't give you a free pass on that. Remember, as long as you have Windows desktop applications, you're going to have to manage Windows somewhere!

How Do You Deliver Old-School Windows Apps as a Service?

If you're on board so far and you want to deliver your old-school Windows desktop applications as a service, how do you go about doing that? From a pure technology perspective, there are a few approaches you can take.

Seamless applications delivered from the data center

In previous chapters, we spent quite a bit of time talking about desktops in the data center. We talked about their advantages (central management, access from anywhere on any device, and good security) and their disadvantages (no offline support, no intense graphics, and client peripheral complexities). What's cool is that we can use the same technologies that deliver desktops from the data center to also deliver single Windows applications from the data center.

We call these "seamless" applications because from the user's perspective, the remote application is seamlessly integrated into the user experience of whatever device they're using. If it's a Windows or Mac computer, the user just clicks on the icon for the applications they want to use, and BAM!—the applications appear and look just like a locally installed applications. The user can resize, move, and ALT+TAB in and out of the remote applications, and the user experience is seamless because the user can't tell where the local desktop ends and the remote applications begin. (Okay, sometimes the user can tell. If the local desktop is a Mac and the remote app is running on Windows, they'll be able to notice the difference in the look and feel. The same is true for a local desktop with Aero enabled connecting to a classic desktop application. In general, though, it all feels integrated.)

The main characteristic of Windows desktop applications delivered seamlessly from the data center is that the user only sees the application's own windows. The user does not see the remote Windows desktop (or any of its elements, like the wallpaper, Start Menu, or icons). In most cases, the full desktop is actually running back in the data center; it's just completely hidden from the user. But since Windows is running behind the scenes, we administrators have to deal with it even when our users do not.

A quick side note: Notice the difference between lowercase "windows" and uppercase "Windows." The latter is the Microsoft Windows OS product, while the former refers to an application's windows that appear on the screen, which the user can move, resize, etc.

If we want to deliver these Windows desktop applications from the data center, there are a few different ways to do it. The most common method is to use the same server-based computing technology that we've been using for fifteen years. That can be done with the built-in features of Windows Server 2008 RDSH (a feature Microsoft has aptly named RemoteApp—get it?), or it can be done by combining Windows with an add-on product like Citrix XenApp, Quest vWorkspace, or Ericom PowerTerm WebConnect.

We can also deliver Windows desktop applications from the data center via VDI technologies. Even though most people think of VDI as a solution for full remote desktops in the data center, it's also possible to use a single VDI instance to deliver a seamless application where the desktop is hidden. This is great for applications that are not compatible with RDSH, but where you still want to deliver them from the data center.

From the user's perspective, there's no real difference between a seamless Windows application coming from an RDSH session or a VDI session. All they know is that they click on an icon and the application appears. But on the back end, seamless apps from VDI require a separate VM for every user, while a single RDSH VM can provide seamless applications to hundreds of users. Most people end up choosing to use RDSH, since it's easier to license and one server can support so many more users.

In addition to RDSH and VDI, there's an emerging crop of a new style of products that can deliver Windows desktop applications from the data center but don't use RDSH or VDI. InstallFree has a product called Nexus that uses their application virtualization technology (more on that later) to run multiple instances of an application on a Windows server, which users can then connect to via an HTML browser client. (It's kind of like RDSH, but without the RDSH component.)

Also, VMware has publicly demonstrated a technology called AppBlast that delivers Windows desktop applications to HTML5 browsers. They haven't explained how it works on the back end, but many people have hypothesized that the applications are not each running in their own VM.

A note about client software

We've detailed a few options you can use if you want to deliver your Windows desktop applications from the data center to your users. One of the realities of this approach is that your users will have to have the proper client software installed on whatever device they're using. Luckily client software exists for just about every platform and device out there. So if you do a search for your application virtualization vendor (Microsoft, Citrix, VMware, Quest, Ericom, etc.) combined with your client platform (Mac, Windows, iOS, Android, Blackberry, Chrome), you'll most likely find the combination you need.

That said, there are certain platforms that aren't supported. (For example, when Amazon's Kindle Fire came out, it was very popular, and it took a while for the vendors to get their Android clients ported over.) The reason this matters is because if you really want to stop worrying about the client devices your users have, this might be an issue for you. (Maybe not. You can also just point them to the supported device list from whichever vendor you chose.)

The other way you can handle "any" device is to use a product with an HTML5 client. Ericom has been shipping one for over a year (AccessNow), and they also sell versions that hook into pure Microsoft environments, VMware View, and Quest vWorkspace. Citrix has demoed a pure HTML5 client, but at the time of this writing, it's only available for Chromebooks.

The HTML5 clients are great because they deliver the data center-based Windows desktops and applications to any device with an HTML5-compliant browser (which is every browser now). So a user on an iPad, iPhone, desktop computer, Android tablet, etc., can just visit a website and after a few clicks, they're using whatever Windows desktop application you want (bearing in mind that data center-based applications always have to be connected and have graphical performance and peripheral limitations).

The bottom line, though, is that regardless of which product and technology you use, it is very possible to deliver your Windows desktop applications as a service from your data center without regard to the client platform or device.

Packaged "virtual" apps running locally on users' client devices

Delivering your Windows desktop applications from the data center is not your only option for delivering them as a service. This is a good thing, because as we've mentioned numerous times before, delivering your Windows desktop applications remotely from the data center has some pretty major disadvantages. (Sure, it's great that you really don't have to worry about the end device, but man, that constant connection requirement and the performance issues can really get you.)

An alternative is to just run your Windows desktop applications locally on the users' client devices. That's what Windows has been doing for the past twenty years, right? The challenge is what we talked about back in Chapter 5, with the fact that Windows desktop applications are hard to install. You can't really deliver an application as a "service" if you have to worry about how it's installed, whether it will conflict, versions of client software, etc.

There is a solution that's the best of both worlds, though, with what's come to be known as application virtualization.

With application virtualization, the Windows application still runs locally on the client device. (This means Windows also has to be running on the client.) The big change versus a traditional Windows desktop is that with application virtualization, the application is packaged in such a way that it doesn't have to be installed on the client—it just runs. Typically the application virtualization vendors build some magic into their products so that the Windows desktop applications that are running in their environments are actually isolated from the Windows OS and from the other desktop applications that are running. This means there's a pretty good chance that the application will work, regardless of what else might be installed on the system.

There are several application virtualization products on the market that do this, the most popular being Microsoft App-V and VMware ThinApp. (Though there are also solutions from Symantec, InstallFree, Endeavors, Citrix, and Spoon.net.) While each product is a bit different, they all do basically the same thing. Let's illustrate how they work using VMware ThinApp as an example.

Imagine you need to deliver Microsoft Word 2010 to your users so that it runs locally on their laptops or desktops. In the traditional way of doing this, you'd run the setup MSI file on each user's computer to get Word installed. (You could either do this manually or automate the setup with a software distribution package.) The Word setup process would copy a bunch of files, make changes to the registry, register a bunch of components and DLLs, etc. As long as that setup process is completely successfully, everything is fine. But of course there's always a chance it won't be successful. Maybe there's an older version of Word that's conflicting, or maybe the user has some other app installed that's preventing Word from installing. The setup is hit-or-miss in this case, and of course the user can't even run Word until the setup process is done, which could take a long time.

Compare that to the ThinApp way of doing things. With ThinApp, you (as the administrator) take the Word installation MSI and associated files and use the ThinApp package creation utility to create a single file package that you then give to your users. That package is a Windows executable (with the file extension .exe), which you might decide to call Word2010.exe. Once that package is created, a user can just click on it, and Word starts running. That's it! (Of course, since that single .exe file actually contains all the bits for the entire Microsoft Word application, it's probably several hundred megabytes in size, but hey, at least it runs!)

The advantage here is that you can say to your users, "Oh, you need Word? Here, take this file and run it." As an administrator, you know for sure it will work. No conflicts. No installation. It just works.

The key downside to this application virtualization technology (whether you use ThinApp or one of the others) is that your users still need to have Microsoft Windows running on their client devices. This isn't going to help you deliver apps to a Mac or an iPad. And your users still need some way to get that huge application file in the first place. (Although it can be cached on the client after it's used the first time so subsequent uses start quickly.) So application virtualization is not the right solution for every scenario. But if you want to provide a Windows application as a service without the downsides of the data center-based application delivery, application virtualization on the client is a great way to do it!

By the way, if this application virtualization sounds amazing and too good to be true, it kind of is! One of the real drawbacks to it is that due to the way the virtualization and isolation works, it's not possible to virtualize every Windows application out there. Some of them are just too specialized or they do too many custom things and the application virtualization engines just can't handle them. (Remember when we talked about how the world of Windows app development is kind of like the Wild West and that anything goes? This is one of the casualties of that.) This means you can't use these application virtualization products across the board, because it's virtually guaranteed that you'll run into some applications that you can't make work.

Let's also not forget that when using application virtualization, your client devices need to be running Windows. So how are you delivering and managing that copy of Windows? Application virtualization saves you the trouble of installing Windows desktops applications—it doesn't save you anything when it comes to managing Windows though.

One extreme way to solve this is to deliver a complete virtual copy of Windows—with the Windows desktop applications preinstalled—that users run on their client device. That way, you guarantee that your Windows desktop applications can run, regardless of whether the user is running Windows, Mac, or Linux, and there's no chance that the user's specific copy of Windows is too screwed up for your virtual application to run. You can even hide the VM's Windows desktop so the user only sees the applications. Crazy? Maybe. Overkill? Maybe. Guaranteed to let Windows desktop applications run regardless of the client OS or its configuration? Yes!

One quick side note about the term "application virtualization." If you take the literal definition of the word "virtualization," it means any time we separate the physical from the logical. So it could be said that the data center-hosted application delivery options, like RDSH and VDI, are technically application virtualization, since they involve users accessing applications from devices where the applications are not installed. We'll give you that. *However*, in the vernacular of the desktop virtualization industry, the term "application virtualization" is used to specifically define the scenario we outlined above, where you have prepackaged applications that run locally on client devices in some sort of isolation bubble.

What About Traditional Windows Desktop Applications on Touch-Based Clients?

Even though you're probably sick of hearing about it, you know that "touch" is all the rage now. iPads and Android tablets are super popular, and Microsoft is focusing on touch in Windows 8 with the new Metro style apps. Unfortunately, for those of us who are responsible for delivering applications to users who want touch, all of our existing Windows desktop applications are not designed for touch. They're designed to be used from devices with keyboards and mice.

While it's great that technology like server-based computing and VDI let us deliver these Windows desktop applications to tablet users, this is not a good experience for them. It works in a pinch, but do users really want to use Windows desktop applications from tablets to do real work? Sure, our RDSH and VDI client software can show the same on-screen keyboard as a native touch-based app, but the old Windows desktop applications use the keyboard a lot (since the designers never expected that the user wouldn't have easy access to a keyboard).

The touch-based interaction is weird, too. Accessing Windows desktop applications via a touch-based client means that the Windows applications use a touch-based mouse emulation mode where users poke at the screen as if they are clicking a mouse. If you've ever tried this, you probably found that your finger is not a good substitute for the clean precision of the mouse pointer, and when you go in for a mouse click, you have maybe a 50/50 chance of hitting the button you want. Inevitably you end up using the tablet's zoom feature to zoom way in on the button you want, and after a few minutes with a Windows desktop application on a tablet, you feel like all you're doing is zooming and panning just to use the thing!

This problem isn't going away anytime soon, since Windows desktop applications will never become 100% touch-based. Sure, the newest developer tools from Microsoft let developers rewrite these apps as Metro style apps, but that's a lot of work, and frankly some apps will always require a keyboard and mouse.

Remember what we said about the "death of the PC" in the previous chapter. While touch is great for people on the go or people lying in bed, the features you need on the go are different than the features you need when you're sitting at a desk. And when you're sitting at a desk, you probably don't want a touch-based app. (Seriously, have you ever tried to touch your screen when sitting at your desk? Your arms get really tired! That's why a mouse is awesome—it lets you rest your arm on the desk while still giving you a precise way to interact with the screen.)

As IT professionals, we understand that users want to use tablets. If our users want to use our apps from their tablets and we're delivering our apps as a service to them, then the users can do it. Just like we said previously, that's one of the nice things about delivering our apps as a service—we don't really care about the devices the users choose. If we're delivering an app that's meant for a desktop with a keyboard and mouse, we'd like to hope that our users choose to connect from a device with a keyboard and mouse. But if they want to use our Windows desktop applications from their iPads and we can deliver them securely, who are we to stop them?

Windows Desktop Applications Can Evolve, But Not All Will

In the next chapter, we're going to look at how the desktop world will evolve beyond Windows desktop applications. But as you can imagine, even though Microsoft claims to embrace a non-Windows application future, of course they don't really want to see that happen! So you can bet that Microsoft is doing everything they can to ensure that the world still sees value in the native Windows-based application.

Throughout this book, we've been using the term "Windows desktop application" to refer to traditional Windows applications that are designed to be used with a keyboard and mouse. Of course, like we just said, this doesn't mean that they must be used with a keyboard and mouse—it's just that they were designed for a keyboard and mouse. (And if you use a Windows desktop application from a touch-based device, your touch is just emulating a mouse click.) Regular Windows apps from the past twenty years fall into what we'd call Windows desktop applications.

New-style touch-based Windows apps written specifically for Windows 8—as we've mentioned a few times—are called "Metro style apps." (Literally, they're called "apps" instead of "applications." So hip and cool!). Metro style apps have a few notable characteristics, including:

- Immersive - Apps fill the whole screen.
- Engaging and alive - Live tiles pull the users in.
- Connected - Apps are designed to be connected and social.
- Interactive and touch-first - Multi-touch and user interaction are key.
- Great in multiple views and form factors - Apps should scale to different size screens.
- Confidence-inspiring - They'll only come from an app store, so they're safe.
- Designed for multitasking – Switching between apps is easy, even in full-screen view.

(This list was copied right from the MSDN article "What are Metro style apps," though the descriptions after the dashes are ours.)

Reading through the list of characteristics of these new Metro style apps, you can see how they're trying to seem new-age and cool, and if that's what Microsoft has to do to compete against Apple and Android, go for it. But you know what doesn't fit into this list? The thousands (or millions?) of existing Windows desktop applications! And unfortunately, converting an existing Windows desktop application to a Metro style app isn't a simple process. Think of the apps you have today? How do you add the connected, multiple form factor, full-screen, tile-based social element to SPSS or Oracle Financials?

The answer, of course, is that you don't. Metro style apps are an option for Windows 8. You still have the ability to deliver regular Windows desktop applications that are boring yet useful.

(To be clear, the version of Windows 8 that runs on ARM-based CPUs will support only third-party apps that are in the Metro style. But that's okay because Windows 8 for ARM is available only for certain tablets. The "normal" version of Windows 8 that runs on x86 and x64 processors will support both Metro style apps and normal Windows desktop applications. So your users can be all social with their multi-touch Twitter-connected restaurant locator and then flip over to the desktop mode to finish their taxes.)

So moving forward, developers will have a choice for which type of Windows app(lication) they want to develop—a Metro style app or a keyboard-and-mouse-based desktop application. (Incidentally, Metro style apps can also run in the data center and be delivered as seamless apps remotely via RDSH or VDI, so as the IT admin, you still get to choose the best delivery method even if the app developer made the decision to go Metro style.)

Creating a Windows Application Delivery Strategy

Now that we've looked at the various options for delivering Windows desktop applications to your users, let's figure out how you can create a strategy to do this. If you take one thing away from this book, let it be that you should forget creating a "desktop virtualization strategy" and instead create a "Windows desktop application strategy." If you get your Windows applications figured out, the desktop part will be easy, (which is great, because then moving from traditional to virtual desktops is nothing more than a form-factor change).

Let's first look at all the questions you have to ask yourself about each application. Then we'll look at how the answers to these questions interrelate to each other. For each of your Windows applications:

- Will the user run Windows on their endpoint? (Either natively or in a VM.)

- Do the application's technical requirements allow it to be delivered from the data center?

- Do your business requirements allow the application to be delivered from the data center? (Users don't need to use it when they're offline, etc.)

- Does this application require the advantages of being delivered from the data center? (Users need to access it from anywhere, from any device, etc.)

- Is this application compatible with RDSH?

- Is it possible to package the application with whatever app virtualization package you've chosen?

- Does the application require a "full" Windows user profile to be loaded in order for it to be used effectively, or does it just need a few registry keys and it's all set?

- Does this application require local integration with other Windows applications? (We're talking about more than "cut & paste" integration. For example, CRM clients might require Word or Excel to generate reports, or a document management application might have to support drag-and-drop from Outlook.)

- Is the endpoint a desktop computer that stays in one place in the office, or is it a laptop?
- Who "owns" the laptop? IT or the user?

The main point of all these questions is to figure out if the application should run locally on a user's client device (App-V, ThinApp, locally installed) or remotely in a data center (RDSH or VDI).

In terms of lowest cost and least change from the way traditional desktops work today, running a Windows desktop application via app virtualization on a user's client device is the cheapest, easiest, and most reliable method for delivering a Windows desktop application. In the perfect world, we'd deliver all our apps this way. But of course this delivery method doesn't work for every app, because:

- Some client devices can't run Windows locally.
- Some applications' requirements dictate that they must be run in the data center.
- Some Windows desktop applications are not compatible with app virtualization.

And of course, running a Windows desktop application locally on a client, even if it's delivered with something like App-V or ThinApp, can be viewed as the "old" way of doing things. Some people just love the idea of not dealing with Windows applications on client devices. (See Bullet No. 2 above.)

Based on these assumptions and the interrelations to these questions, we've developed the following flowchart that can help you whittle down the various delivery options for the application in question. (Remember that you'll run through this once for each Windows application that you have.)

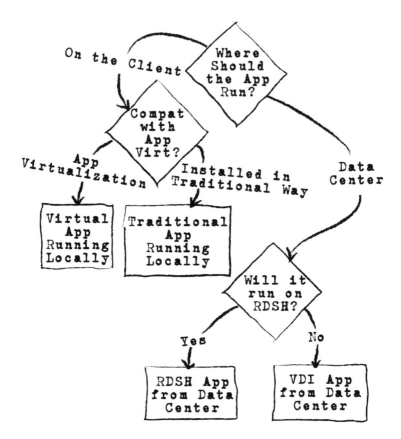

Keep in mind that this flowchart is just something to provide another data point to help you with your decision. It shouldn't be viewed as dogmatic. For example, if you have twenty applications and you discover that you can deliver nineteen via VDI, it might make sense to deliver the last one via VDI, too. In that case, you'd be saving the complexity of not having to add another delivery method even though that other method theoretically makes more sense for that final app. Or, you might have one application that makes the most sense running in the data center and another that seems like it should be run locally on a client. But if a user needs to be able to drag-and-drop files between those two applications, you can't have one local and one remote, so you'd have to sacrifice something to run both the apps in the same place.

What About the Data?

There's a guy from Boston named Tim Mangan (a friend of ours) who's probably bursting out of his seat after reading this chapter. Tim is known for a lot of things (like being an App-V guru and a ten-time BriForum speaker), but one thing it seems like Tim is always talking about is data. "Apps are worthless without their data!" is one of his favorite phrases.

Certainly there's some truth to that. For as much as we've talked about how the "desktop" doesn't really do anything and that the apps are what IT really cares about, an argument could be made that the apps can't do anything either without the data they do it to.

Data comes in a lot of different forms—databases, web feeds, folders full of files—but almost all of it is useless without the applications to manipulate them. So we take the position that both the data and the applications are equally important.

Perhaps the only real difference is that data is automatically platform-independent, which means it's relatively easy to get the data to wherever the user needs it. (On their device, in the cloud, in a Windows share—no problem!) The challenge, of course, is making sure that there's an app that can deal with the data where the user needs it. So that's why we're mostly focusing on apps now. (We'll revisit this topic in Chapter 11, when we discuss how to put everything together.)

What About the User Settings?

The final bit of the Windows experience we have to talk about is the user settings. We touched on this a bit earlier, and we'll cover it more later on, but as long as we're talking about converting Windows into a service, we should include the user settings here.

You probably know that Windows has something called a user profile, which is, roughly speaking, the collection of registry settings, user configurations, and data files that a specific user needs for their Windows environment to be complete.

In the context of Windows desktop applications, the Windows user profile needs to be loaded into the same copy of Windows where the applications run. So in a traditional desktop computing environment, the applications run locally on the user's desktop and the user profiles and settings are on that same desktop.

In the case of Windows desktop applications that live in the data center (which are provided as a service to users via RDSH or VDI), the Windows user profile also lives in the data center and is loaded in the remote host when the user connects. You might think, "But the user settings don't matter because there is no background. Who cares if the user has a kitten wallpaper if they'll never see it?" The challenge is that there's a lot of under-the-hood stuff that these settings control, including things like application configuration settings, printer connections, and drive mappings.

There's this idea in the industry that we must evolve beyond Windows user profiles and into something called a "user workspace" or "user environment" or some such thing. The basic idea behind these things is that they take the concept of the Windows user profile (the users' ability to customize their experience, save configuration settings, etc.) and apply that in a cross-platform way so that the user settings truly follow the user, regardless of where he or she connects or what platform is used. In theory, a user should have to say "This is my email server" only once, and then whenever they launch a mail client, it should just work—regardless of whether it's the iPad's mail app or Android mail or Microsoft Outlook running in a remote RDSH session. We agree. But again, that's beyond the scope of delivering Windows apps as a service. (In fact, the user profile that's part of the Windows app as a service should just plug into that great user workspace concept.) So again, we'll discuss that in a few other chapters.

Chapter 10

Moving Beyond Windows Applications

U<small>P UNTIL THIS POINT, MOST OF OUR FOCUS</small> in this book has been about Windows desktops and Windows applications. In fact, we spent the whole last chapter talking about how you could convert legacy Windows desktop applications into something that you could deliver as a service.

As you know, though, there are a lot of other types of apps in the world in addition to Windows applications, and that's what we're going to look at in this chapter.

Alternatives to Windows Desktop Applications?

What's wrong with Windows desktop applications? Why do we even care about alternatives? We already talked about how difficult it is to deal with the fact that Windows desktop applications can do whatever they want to the operating system, leave files all over the place, and be a huge pain to install. And of course, Windows desktop applications require Windows! (That's like saying, "Hi, old friend, can I stay at your house for the weekend?" And then once your friend says yes, you add, "Great! I'm also going to bring my whole family, I'm going to eat your food, and I'm going to mess up your house.")

Imagine the alternate possibilities: there are no conflicts, data is isolated in one location, apps are easy to install and remove, and they can run anywhere. It sounds great! You know this world is available now, right?

There are plenty of alternative application architectures besides Windows, including device-native apps from app stores, classic web apps, and new-style HTML5 apps. And while that world of alternative apps used to take a backseat to Windows desktop applications, we're now seeing that many mainstream apps are available in these alternative formats. (Can we even call these "alternative" anymore?)

When looking at these alternative application formats, we also have to look at how and where they store their information and data. After all, it's possible to have a local device-native app that requires the cloud to do anything, just as it's possible to have a native HTML5 app run locally (and offline!) on your client device.

Let's explore the other non-Windows desktop application platforms that are out there today.

Native Apps from App Stores

One of the major characteristics of Windows desktop applications is that they're specifically written and compiled to run on Windows platforms. (And, in fact, they have to be specifically compiled to run on certain processor families. Windows ARM apps won't run on Windows running on an x86 processor, etc.) These types of applications are what we call "native" applications because they run natively on a platform or device. So Windows desktop applications are native Windows apps, Mac OS X applications are native Mac apps, etc.

Mobile devices can also have native apps. You install iOS apps onto your iPhone, Android apps onto your Android phone, etc.

But there's one major difference between native Windows apps and native iOS apps—iOS apps can only be installed from the Apple App Store. So the apps are iOS native apps, but you can't just go out and get them from anywhere—you have to get them from Apple. Other platforms have app stores, too. Android has the Android Market. Blackberry has App World. Windows phones get apps from the Windows Phone Marketplace.

App stores aren't limited to just mobile devices and tablets. Apple introduced a Mac App Store in early 2011 that's just like the iOS App Store except it's for Mac desktop apps. And Windows 8 includes a Windows Store, which will be the only way users can get Metro style apps.

(By the way, Apple has tried to trademark the term "App Store." They haven't succeeded yet, though, with others claiming the term is generic. Throughout this book, we will use "app store" to mean the generic concept of an app store. If we're talking about Apple's specific app store, we'll say "Apple App Store.")

Benefits of app store apps

There are a few things that all of these native apps have in common, regardless of which platform they're for or whether they're mobile or desktop apps.

App store apps are curated

One of the problems that plagued computers in the past (Windows included) was that it was too easy for users to get spyware and viruses, and it was too easy for poorly written apps to crash or cause the system to be unstable.

App stores avoid that because the applications they include are curated—in other words, there are people running the app store who test, review, and approve the apps before they're made available for users to install. The idea (in theory anyway) is that this prevents unsafe, malicious, and problematic apps from being made available, and users can happily install whatever they want with confidence.

The curated list also means that there's a single central repository of every application available. So if a user is looking for an awesome Euchre app, for example, they can search in just one place instead of spending hours and hours scouring the depths of Google.

App store apps install themselves

When a user wants to install an app from an app store, they just click the install button, and that's it! With native applications that don't come from app stores, it seems like you have to click Next, Next, Next forever. Then they need your name, your license number, the installation location, the options you want—it just never ends!

Contrast that to apps from app stores. Click. Done. They don't ask you a bunch of questions because they know who you are, they know what device you have, and they know where to put their files.

App store apps don't conflict with each other

Another complexity of native Windows desktop applications that we've talked about before is they have the potential to conflict with each other. Remember all the things that Windows desktop applications do that make them difficult to virtualize? Everything that these new native apps from app stores do is the exact opposite. Native apps are limited to certain sets of APIs and all the files stay in one place.

App store apps are always up to date

Since the native apps from app stores only run in their specific area and have a central point of management (the app store), it's possible for app store apps to automatically update themselves. So now, instead of searching the Internet for all the latest updates to all your apps, the app store pushes update notifications (and possibly the updates themselves) right to you.

App store apps are automatically licensed and secured

Piracy has always been a problem in the traditional world of applications. But with apps that come from app stores, the user logs into the app store itself. Then when they install an application, the app store knows who the user is. This is great because (1) the user doesn't have to enter his or her contact information or mess with license keys, and (2) the app store framework provides anti-piracy controls so that one user can't copy his apps to another user's device. (Although we should point out that people who want to pirate software will always find ways to break this. The point is that this capability is built into the platform instead of every app having to do it on its own.)

Drawbacks of app store apps

While there are a lot of cool things about app stores, there's an equally long list of things that people don't like about them, specifically:

Apps can't access certain things on the hardware or do some things

The biggest complaint about the app stores that are controlled by the big vendors is that the vendors get to specify what the apps in the store are allowed to do. They decide which APIs can and cannot be used and which features apps will be allowed to have. If an app developer finds a backdoor way to do something, the app won't be approved for inclusion in the store.

There are a lot of examples of this. For example, Apple doesn't allow apps that duplicate the built-in functionality of iOS, which is why you can't get a Safari browser replacement. And they don't allow apps that replace standard interface elements, which is why you can't get the Swype keyboard for iOS, even though everyone who uses it thinks it's awesome.

Apple also has a rule that all in-app purchases must be made through their app store (which takes a cut of the sales), so that's why you can get the Kindle book reading app but you can't buy books from it.

App store owners have ultimate authority

The other big problem people have with the big vendor app stores is that while it's cool that those app stores are curated, it's unfortunate that we're not the ones doing the curating! In other words, if an app developer has an idea for an awesome app, they can write and submit the app to the app store, but the app store vendor could decide for whatever reason that they're not going to approve it. And if you don't like it? That's too bad.

Apps can be pulled on the app store vendors' terms

In addition to the app store vendors controlling what goes in the app store, they can pull stuff out of the app store at any time for any reason. There's no court of appeals or due process.

There's a paper trail for user installations

In general, it's nice for users to be able to download whatever apps they want without anyone being able to track what they do. But when they're getting apps from a central app store, even the free apps they download are tied back to their own user account. That data can be stolen, subpoenaed, and otherwise made available to the world.

Even custom in-house apps have to go through the app store

One of the realities about the big app stores is that even major software vendors have to play by the app store owner's rules. We hear huge, multibillion-dollar companies like Citrix and VMware say things like, "Well, our awesome new desktop virtualization client is ready to go, so it will be available whenever Apple approves it." How lame is that?

The same is true when companies write their own internal apps that they then need to distribute via the app store. It's weird that some smart phone vendor half a world away has total control over when you can release the new version of your own internally developed app to your users.

App store vendors take a cut of sales

All these great features of curated app store apps come at a cost—literally. Apple, for example, takes 30% of the sale price of every app as a commission.

Having an app store doesn't guarantee compatibility

One of the misnomers of the world of curated app stores is that all the apps will "just work." (Actually, didn't we say that a few pages back?) While that's true for apps within an app store, how many different app stores are out there? We talked about iOS, Blackberry, Android, and Windows. But what about different app stores on the same platform? The Amazon Kindle Fire runs Android, but it's a different app store (and not compatible) with the general Google Android Market. And each of the carriers has their own app store. Can you run an Android app from the Sprint app store on a Verizon phone? How about on a Kindle Fire? Who knows? And you thought native apps were just supposed to work!

Actually, there are some special difficulties for Android applications in addition to all the different app stores. Fragmentation means there's a large variety of different versions of Android devices in the world today. Developers have to consider widely varying screen dimensions, processing power, and hardware features. The results are some of the same problems that arise for applications developed for Windows. Some hardware/app combinations will be great, some will work just okay, and some combinations will just be miserable to use. As a result, developers have to make compromises and put effort into ensuring their applications can accommodate a wide variety of configurations.

So while it's cool that Android is open source, this means that ultimately anyone is able to use it however they want. But how is it possible that a single Android app is going to work well on a four-inch phone, a ten-inch tablet, a thirteen-inch Android laptop, and a twenty-two-cubic-foot refrigerator? There's no way that any app can work well on all of these things.

Native Apps Outside the Boundaries of the App Store

Now that we've looked at the pros and cons of native curated apps from app stores, it's worth taking a few minutes to think about what happens if we take the app store out of the picture. You might be thinking, "What? Isn't that just like the regular Windows desktop applications that we just spent the last 100 pages trying to get away from?"

Yes.

But now that we've looked at the downsides of the app stores, suddenly the Wild West of uncurated applications doesn't look so bad, does it?

Of course every platform has different technical characteristics that define what you can and cannot do outside of the app store.

Microsoft Windows running on x86/x64 processors can run traditional Windows desktop applications no problem. If you want to run Metro style apps, though, they have to come from the app store. Microsoft Windows running on ARM processors will only run apps from the app store (assuming someone hasn't cracked it yet).

iOS devices can only run apps from the app store. The only alternative is to jailbreak it (essentially installing a cracked copy of the device's OS, which isn't controlled by Apple). That's possibly illegal and definitely not something that Apple likes.

Running non-app store apps on most Android devices is pretty easy, as there's a simple check box that the user can click to allow them to download apps from the Internet that aren't monitored, delivered, or controlled by Google. You can also run non-app store apps on your Kindle Fire, but you have to "root" it (which is where you crack the OS and install an unsupported version).

Mac OS X (Apple's operating system for desktops and laptops) is interesting. As we mentioned before, there is an app store. But so far, people have been able to also run non-app store apps they found on their own. But OS X 10.8 (called Mountain Lion) contains a security setting where you can restrict the system to only run app store apps. Today, that will be an option that anyone with admin rights can change, but people have started wondering if Apple will somehow force everyone to get everything from the app store in the future.

An interesting footnote to this conversation about all the jailbreaking and rooting of various devices is that doing so not only opens up these systems to run whatever apps users want—it also means that these devices are susceptible to rogue applications, viruses, and malware. So now we have security and malware protection software for all these supposedly secure platforms. After all this, it's just like Windows again!

Web Apps

Now we know that despite the many benefits of platform-native apps from app stores, there are a lot of drawbacks and complexities. The alternatives to native apps are platform-independent apps. As the name implies, platform-independent apps are those that can run on any platform. The classic example is Adobe Flash. If you have the Flash player on your device, you can use the same Flash app, regardless of the OS or device you have. (In a sense, the Flash player becomes your application's runtime instead of your OS.)

The other classic platform-independent application framework is the web. Web apps are as easy as (1) you need a web browser, and (2) you point it to the site. At first glance it seems like web-based apps can solve the platform fragmentation, deployment, and conflict issues.

This all sounds great, but we all know web apps are often limited and sometimes cause quite a bit of pain. On the other hand, we've also started hearing more about Web 2.0 or HTML5 apps, which are supposed to feel more like local apps. So let's take a closer look at each of these.

Old-style web apps

Web apps have been making the same promises for going on twenty years—they render client software unnecessary and as a result can be accessed from anywhere. The problem is that for a long time (and still true today), web-based apps have simply been a poorer experience. (Think about Outlook Web Access versus the desktop version of Outlook.) So it's really been a trade-off between the "anywhere access" of web apps versus the richness of native apps.

Ever since Netscape released a web browser that supported JavaScript back in 1995, web standards consortiums and web developers have been trying to close the gap between web apps and native apps, adding more capabilities to the web and writing more powerful web apps.

Unfortunately, competition between browser makers in the early days meant that each browser implemented supposed "standards" a bit differently. Add to that the fact that early browsers were stuffed full of plug-ins and extensions and we very quickly ended up in a world where these allegedly platform-independent web apps would only work with specific browser, platform, and plug-in combinations. (Have you ever compared Outlook Web Access from Internet Explorer on Windows to Chrome on the Mac? It is not the same thing!)

This craziness culminated in 2001 when Microsoft released Internet Explorer 6 (IE6). So excited to enable these new web apps to be as "powerful" as native apps, Microsoft designed IE6 to all websites to run code at the same level of privilege as a logged-in user, which meant that web apps could have access to local file systems and other processors and resources. This was great for the makers of web apps, since it meant they could be more powerful than ever. It was equally great for the creators of viruses and malware! Nevertheless, the "power" of IE6 resulted in a lot of enterprise web apps being created that will only run in it.

The end result of all of these issues is that web apps had so many specific client and browser requirements that they're just as heavy as any other platform-native app. The only difference is that the "platform" was now the browser with its associated plug-ins rather than the base OS. This is where we learned that "browser-based" and "browser-independent" are not the same thing.

In perhaps the ultimate example of this, the folks in Oracle's VDI group once told us that many of the web versions of Oracle's own products are so complicated that the easiest way to demo them at trade shows is to have separate VMs with all the correct browser builds and configurations, which they connect to from

Sun Ray thin clients. That's easier than trying to rewrite everything in a browser-independent way.

The irony here is that Oracle is addressing the complexity of their own web apps the same way we're advocating for you to deal with Windows desktop applications—build some copies in your data center and deliver them to your users via RDSH or VDI. You might as well figure it out now because they're both going to be around for a long time!

Taken together, these characteristics of web apps meant they were relegated to be more simple, less rich, and occasional-use applications. Throughout the 2000s, due to the complex browser requirements and limited functionality, no one really expected that web apps would replace the rich experience of native apps anytime soon.

HTML5 and the new style of web apps

The past few years have ushered in a resurgence of popularity for web applications, some of which are so good that it's even hard to tell they're running in a browser! This is another major industry trend that is the subject of dozens of books, but for our purposes here, let's look at a few of the key reasons.

HTML5

Most newly created web apps are being built around HTML5. HTML5 eliminates many of the issues created by older web apps, mostly because it's becoming a very widely accepted standard. (We're not really sure how the stars aligned to make that happen, but even Microsoft's Internet Explorer 10 is said to be 100% HTML5-compliant.)

HTML5 also supports some new powerful tags, including one called "canvas" that allows the web app to have pixel-level control over what the browser renders. (This is what allowed Ericom and Citrix to create the web versions of their VDI clients. They're not using browser plug-ins like the old days—they have literally written the entire client as an HTML5 native web app that can run on any HTML5 browser.)

Pixel-level access to the client screen is done through browser APIs accessed via the web app's JavaScript. In addition to APIs for the canvas, HTML5 specifies them for GPU access, videos, audio support, offline data caching, web storage, drag-and-drop, etc.

New versions of browsers every six weeks

The recent trend in the world of web browsers is to release them often. Google Chrome advanced from Version 8 to 16 in the course of 2011 alone. Firefox adopted a similar schedule midyear, going from Version 5 to 9 between June and December 2011.

In a world of web apps, the browser becomes the new application runtime, and having new browsers every few weeks means that web apps will constantly be able to access additional and more powerful features.

Web apps pick up where the app stores locked them out

Another element that's driving the adoption of HTML5 apps is that web pages, generally speaking, aren't curated. When Steve Jobs announced the iPhone SDK and App Store in 2008, many people were upset that Apple would have to approve their apps. Apple's response to this was that "web apps" (meaning websites visited from the phone) don't have to be approved, so anyone who doesn't want to use the iPhone SDK or submit their apps to the App Store can just write a web app.

Web apps are not platform-specific

Just like the web apps of the past decade, today's HTML5 web apps are not platform-specific. So if you're a developer with limited resources, what would you rather do—write iOS, Android, Blackberry, and Windows Mobile versions of your app, or instead write a single HTML5 web version? Sure, maybe that web version can't do quite as much as a native app. (For example, a native iOS app can leverage push notifications and the Game Center, while a web app cannot.) But web apps also don't have to deal with all the chicanery of the platform's app store.

Web apps can still "feel" natural

Many people are still nervous about web apps because they believe that web apps don't "feel" like regular native applications. (We blame you, Outlook Web Access from Firefox!) But properly written HTML5 apps really change that. Install the native Gmail iOS app on your iPhone and then use the iPhone's browser to visit the Gmail website. Now show both of these to someone who doesn't know which is which and see if they can guess.

Gmail is actually a great example of what's possible in a web app. You can visit the same Gmail website from a mobile phone, a tablet, and a desktop, and all three have a very different, form-factor-appropriate look and feel. And if you create a browser shortcut on your device or desktop for Chrome, after a week you'll forget that you're even using a web app. (Well, until you go offline. Offline support for the Gmail web app is only available via the Chrome browser, and then you need an extension, so we're not quite there yet!)

Web apps aren't limited to just mobile

Many of the examples of successful new-style HTML5 web apps are shown on mobile devices. That's fine, but don't forget that all these capabilities are available on desktops and laptops, too. Everything we're talking about for HTML5 web apps is valid regardless of form factor.

Most consumer websites are highly interactive

One of the aspects driving this new level of interactivity in the browser is that all of today's new consumer-oriented companies have very interactive websites. Call it Web 2.0 or whatever, but nowadays it seems like no major application-oriented websites actually load "pages" anymore. Just think about Gmail, Twitter, LinkedIn, or Facebook. If you took away the chrome of the browser, you wouldn't even know you were using a web app. (The "chrome" is everything surrounding the main window, including the address bar, buttons, frame, etc.) They all have multiple elements that load on demand, we now have infinite scrolling with new content just appearing as you continue to scroll down, you can drag files into web apps to upload them, etc.

All of these sites have contributed to an environment where users just expect that web apps work like this. These are two-way interactive applications, not one-way pages that users simply read.

Users have grown accustomed to doing real work in web apps

A few years ago, end users and IT admins shared the same opinion about web apps—it was nice that they could be accessed from anywhere, but they provided a sub-par experience. But just as web applications have slowly evolved to be more interactive, users have grown accustomed to using these new apps.

Now we're to the point that if IT says, "Can we borrow your laptop to install this new app?" the user's reaction will be an eye roll followed by, "Why isn't this just a web app?"

Every year that passes leads to more apps moving to the web. In fact, we're writing this entire book in Google Docs, and at our company, we've almost completely stopped using Word and Excel in favor of Google's web versions. (We still use native PowerPoint, though.)

Downsides to new HTML5 web app platforms

Not everything is rosy when it comes to these new web apps. First we have the problem that all the examples cited above are new apps that the developers specifically wrote for HTML5. But how does that fit into the past twenty years of Windows apps that you're dealing with in your company? Those aren't being magically converted (which is why we looked at trying to deliver them as a service in the last chapter).

We also have the problem that the browser makers are updating their browsers every six weeks. Hopefully your users will have their computers set to automatically download the latest versions, but really we have the same problem we've always had. If there's a security problem that you need to address, how do you find out which users are using which browsers? And how do you deal with an inventory report that shows you have fifteen different browsers in use?

(Firefox is trying to address this at some level by creating Extended Support Release versions that they'll support with bug fixes and security updates for a full year. Firefox 10, for example, is one of these, which is why it's still supported even as Firefox 11 support is deprecated in the wake of Firefox 12.)

Also, web browsers don't have full access to the native device's capabilities. (This is a good thing. Remember IE6?) Even though browser makers are continuously adding and extending their APIs, HTML5 apps still can't do as much as native apps can. (Maybe the HTML5 app can't access some advanced hardware features, or it can't deliver notifications in the background, since the app isn't running when the browser page is closed.)

The final challenge for HTML5 apps is that since there are so many different form factors of clients with fully compliant HTML5 browsers, it can be difficult for a single application to reorient itself for whatever device the user chooses. How can a single application target tiny, medium, and large screens, maybe with a keyboard, maybe without, maybe with a mouse, maybe with multi-touch fingers? Even though the back-end web app code can work on every device, who has the time to plan for so many different interfaces?

Who wins? HTML5 web apps or native apps?

To be honest, for most enterprise apps, HTML5 will probably be "good enough." Heck, most of your current enterprise apps are probably traditional web apps, so moving to the richer experience of HTML5 would actually be an upgrade.

The main problem is that native apps are guaranteed to work, while HTML5 might or might not. But native apps will only work on devices of the right platform, and if you're controlling the platform, then you can also control which browser the user has for HTML5 apps. (Plus, most HTML5 apps will work on all HTML5 browsers, even if they're with reduced functionality when the preferred browser isn't available.)

Is the browser the new OS?

The incredible features of browser-based web applications are enabled because HTML5 and JavaScript are essentially turning the browser into a mini operating system. Applications are interpreted at runtime, which is less efficient than compiled applications, although more advanced browsers take on this problem by actually precompiling parts of applications. The end result is that browsers give us a third space for applications to run in (in addition to server-hosted and local native).

Unfortunately, at this cutting-edge level, application features and performance become client-dependent again, because the applications rely more strongly on browser capabilities. Google Chrome and Firefox feature these advanced capabilities, but if you're stuck using Internet Explorer or Safari, then you're out of luck.

Runtime Location Versus Data Location

When talking about device-native apps and web apps, there's bound to be some confusion. Web apps work offline? Device-native apps are worthless without an Internet connection? What is this crazy world? You have cloud apps, cloud-enabled web apps, native apps, cloud-enabled native apps—there can be all sorts of combinations, because where and how data is stored is completely independent from its runtime architecture.

In other words, yes, we say that native apps are cloud apps, and browser-based apps don't even need to be connected to the Internet!

Let's look at a few examples of how applications can combine local and external data with different runtime scenarios:

- Native apps can store all their data in the cloud, so the app is local and native, but it doesn't really do anything without the Internet (examples: Microsoft Outlook, iOS Mail client, iMessage).

- Native apps run locally and store their data locally (examples: Microsoft Word, Photoshop).

- A traditional web app runs in a browser. All of its data is stored in the cloud or on the web. Offline access is not supported (examples: BrianMadden. com, TripIt, Concur, Salesforce).

- An HTML5 web app runs in a browser. It stores all of its information in the cloud but keeps a subset cached locally on the client so it can work offline (examples: mail.google.com, Amazon Kindle Cloud Reader, NYTimes).

Web apps versus SaaS apps

One final note about all these new non-Windows apps. There's a difference between web apps and SaaS apps. Web apps (or HTML5 apps) refers to the technology that's being used, while SaaS (remember it's "software as a service") describes the business model that a company uses to consume the app. It's possible for a company to buy and host a web or HTML5 app internally. In that case, we'd say that they have a web app even though it's not SaaS. It's also possible that SaaS apps are not based on web app technologies. (At lot of companies use hosted Exchange, and the client the users install is the regular Windows desktop version of Outlook.)

Of course in many cases, SaaS apps are web apps, but remember that they don't have to be, and vice versa.

The End Result

Luckily for our future job security, people will be debating the virtues of web apps versus native apps for many years to come. At this point, we can see that they both have a place, and most likely your current environment is a mixture of both.

So now that we've looked at how to deliver Windows desktop applications as a service and have dug into the details of how web apps work, let's look at how you can pull this all together to create a desktop and application delivery strategy for your company.

Chapter 11

Putting It All Together

E ARLY ON IN THIS BOOK WE TALKED ABOUT HOW IT is more about delivering applications than delivering desktops. Sure, for the past twenty years we've focused on Windows *desktops*, but that's because we needed the desktop to get our applications. The last few chapters have made it clear that you can deliver *applications*—whether they're Windows, web apps, or HTML5—to users regardless of the client platform or type of device they're using. (With the caveat being that some application types are more appropriate for certain types of clients.)

Once you figure out how to deliver the individual apps, the next step is to turn it back into a "desktop" by gluing together the common authentication, identity management, app stores, client devices, user settings, and data sync. That's what we're going to look at in this chapter.

The Challenge: Hooking All These Apps Together

Ten years ago, since just about all of our applications ran on Windows, we didn't have to talk about hooking anything together at all. We just gave our users Windows desktops that ran our Windows applications, and that was pretty much it. That Windows desktop had all the "glue" we needed to hook our Windows applications together, including common:

- Authentication (you can log into Windows once and run the apps you need)
- User interface (users can resize Windows, move them around, and Alt+Tab between them)
- App launcher (just click on the icon in the Start Menu or on the desktop)
- Provisioning target (you can deliver new applications to users by installing them on their desktops or pushing shortcuts out)
- Mechanism for applications to integrate with each other (cut, copy, and paste, OLE linking, drag-and-drop, etc.)
- Look and feel to the user interface for all the elements of the applications (users can set font sizes, button colors, menu sizes, etc., in a single Windows-wide setting, which is then applied to every element of every application)
- Access to user-based and system-wide configuration options (time zone, spelling dictionaries, time and date formats, etc.)

Of course letting the Windows desktop provide all these features only worked when all our applications were Windows desktop applications. But when web apps started to enter the scene, the commonality we had with Windows started to break down. With web apps:

- All web apps are channeled through a single Windows desktop application: the web browser. This makes the general "feel" of navigation weird. (Users can Alt+Tab through all their desktop applications, but all the web apps are clumped together in a single browser. And tabs haven't fixed this yet.)

- Moving between multiple web apps means that users have to move multiple instances of the web browser around.

- If we want to give users access to a new web app, we have to use that app's system to set up the user account.

- Provisioning the web app for a user means sending them a shortcut or telling them to launch the browser and then go to a URL.

- Web apps don't have "true" integration with each other or Windows desktop applications.

- Each browser or web app renders its buttons and UI elements using its own settings. Every app looks different.

- Every web app has to maintain personalization settings on its own. Users have to specify that they're in the GMT-8 time zone for each app one by one.

Of course we try to get around these limitations as much as we can. We create Windows shortcuts to URLs and distribute those to users and put them in the users' Start Menus and leverage simple copying and pasting as our "integration" between multiple different apps. While this was fine when we only had a few web apps, as web app use grew, the ultimate experience for the user became very disjointed. There's just nothing that ties the various web apps together.

The same applies to users accessing web apps from tablets. Users are able to launch native tablet apps by touching the icon, but for web apps, they have to launch the browser and then type in the URL or go to the bookmark. And even if the user creates an icon for the browser shortcut, the web app still doesn't feel the same as a native app. (And don't forget the browser compatibility issues that we talked about in Chapter 10.)

The final challenge with web apps is there's no single place to provision and configure users. For most Windows desktop applications, it's as simple as adding the user to a group in Active

Directory. But for all these external web apps, someone needs to log into each app one by one to add each user.

While most people's initial thoughts about web apps are that they're easy to deliver (just give the user the link), the reality is that the proliferation of them actually makes things pretty complex. In fact, there's a very real chance that web-based SaaS apps are actually making things worse for companies. For example, it might be great when your company moves to an enterprise web-based corporate expense app, but now you have to manage user accounts and passwords and their configuration with that SaaS vendor in addition to managing the internal Active Directory. Want to use Salesforce? Great! Except now that's another vendor's product that requires discrete management. Since all of these SaaS apps come from different suppliers, they're all managed separately. When a new employee comes on board, it could take a week to get all the accounts and access configured properly in all the various systems. The same goes for when an employee leaves.

What are we looking for?

Despite these complexities, the popularity of web and SaaS apps continues to increase, so we have to deal with them regardless. To make Windows and web apps work well together, we need to accomplish a few goals:

Single app-launching interface

One simple way to integrate web apps with Windows desktop applications is to deliver both types via a single user interface. If your users have full Windows desktops, push out the web app icons to the Start Menu (or wherever else they launch their Windows apps). If you deliver Windows applications via some kind of web interface like Citrix XenApp or Quest vWorkspace, deliver the shortcuts to the individual web apps via that web interface.

Single sign-on

The next level of integration is to make it so your users don't have to enter separate usernames and passwords to access different web apps. Luckily, there are a few different ways to do this.

The most basic option is to use some kind of "password stuffer"—a little piece of software that runs on a user's device that automatically submits his or her credentials into the HTML form fields of the website the user is connecting to. There are many consumer-oriented products that do this (LastPass, 1Password, and KeePass, for example), as well as several enterprise-level products that IT can more easily manage. Password stuffers work well at a basic level, but they can't handle advanced scenarios like two-factor authentication.

Another single sign-on option is to use the more advanced capabilities of web apps where they can reach into your company's corporate directory (like AD) to find out if a user should be granted access to a certain asset. There are several newer standards for this, like SAML, OAuth, and OpenID. The nitty-gritty details of this are beyond the scope of this book, but the basic idea is that even if you keep all your user accounts in an internal AD environment, it's still possible to allow third-party cloud-hosted web apps to securely leverage your existing system for authentication. The technology that handles this is slick, with the only main problem being you have to find out which web apps use the same type of delegated authentication that your internal system can offer, as this whole concept is pretty new.

Single provisioning

In what might be described as the Holy Grail of web app integration, some people are now looking at ways to integrate the provisioning (and deprovisioning) of web app users with internal corporate users. For example, if your company uses Box (formerly called Box.net) for cloud-based file syncing and sharing, in the current way of working, someone from your company has to log into the Box website and create the user account for each user who needs access. But if there were some type of integrated provisioning, getting a user's Box account setup could be as simple as adding them to the group in your internal AD. The two systems would then talk, and the Box account would be created automatically. Disabling the user's AD account would in turn remove access to Box.

How vendors attempt to solve these integration problems

While traditional password-stuffing utilities have been around for a while, we're just now starting to see new products that can mix web apps and Windows desktop applications, including single points of access, single sign-on, and the provisioning of external web applications for internal users. There are several vendors and products in this space, including some names familiar to desktop virtualization folks, like VMware's Horizon Application Manager, Citrix's Cloud Gateway Enterprise, and Quest Software's Webthority.

Though the exact architecture of each product differs, the concepts driving them are the same. They all want to aggregate, control, and deliver all app formats, including:

- Windows desktop applications delivered from the data center
- Windows desktops delivered from the data center
- Windows desktop applications streamed down to clients and executed locally
- Internet web app links
- External web/SaaS app links
- Native mobile apps

Application management solutions

As we said previously, these new integration products are just now emerging. (We don't even really know what to call them exactly. Citrix uses the term "universal service broker," which seems as good as anything.) What we do know is that it feels like we're dealing with a lot of "Version 1" products. (Even products with higher version numbers are new to this kind of capability.)

VMware, Citrix, Quest, and the other providers are really pushing these things, and we expect their capabilities will advance quickly. We also expect that more SaaS and web app providers will create or support whatever provisioning APIs or standards are needed, and more of us will have federated authentication systems in our companies that can do "real" single sign-on instead of resorting to wonky password-stuffing techniques. So while this whole thing might be a slow march that takes years to shake out, every month will be better than the last.

We also assume that the makers of these universal service brokers will continue to create native clients for all platforms. (Citrix seems to be ahead in this area as of this writing.) So your users will be able to have a native app manager for iOS, Android, Windows, Mac, Blackberry, etc., that will aggregate their Windows desktop applications, device native apps, and web app shortcuts on whatever device they have. We'll also see more intelligence that correlates a single application across multiple delivery factors and platforms. For example, as the administrator, you'd be able to say, "This user needs Salesforce." Then if that user were using an iPhone, the app manager agent would ensure that the iOS native Salesforce app was installed. If the user were on a desktop-style client with a keyboard and mouse, the app manager agent would deliver the link to the real HTML5 Salesforce app, etc. The user wouldn't have to go get the Salesforce app for every platform he or she connected from, and they'd never have to manually log into Salesforce, as the authentication would be federated to your own AD system.

User personality integration

While you're thinking about bridging the gap between Windows, web, and SaaS apps, we'd love it if you could also think about how you can extend the user personality and settings across platforms. The vendors (AppSense, RES Software, and Scense especially) have started talking about this as their long-term vision, though their products just don't offer those capabilities today.

The ultimate goal would be to abstract and then inject user settings and preferences independently from the application delivery itself. A simple example would be Microsoft Word. If a user adds a word to his custom dictionary from Word running on his Mac desktop, that word should also be added to the dictionary in a copy of Word running centrally in an RDSH session. The same could be true for mail settings, wallpapers, photo locations, data files, account numbers, which hand the user likes the mouse in, etc.

Unfortunately, we're just barely starting to integrate ways of managing and delivering different types of apps—dynamically injecting user preferences is still a long way off. But it's still worth keeping in the back of your mind.

Corporate app stores

We've already written quite a bit about the various app stores for the different platforms out there. (Apple iOS App Store, Mac App Store, Android Market, Blackberry App World, the Windows Store, etc.) Really, they're nothing too fancy—just a way to let users pick out new apps themselves instead of having to call the help desk.

The new trend we're seeing is that corporations are starting to create their own app stores. You could probably argue that Microsoft SMS 2.0 in the 1990s had an "app store," though back then, it required the users to hunt it down via the Systems Management icon in the Control Panel. But once there, they could click on a package name and it would be automatically installed onto their computer.

In today's world, whether you decide to run your own app store or integrate with an existing platform's store, there are several things that app stores have in common that differentiate them from the traditional way of deploying applications. Specific characteristics of an app store include:

- One location for users to go to see all the apps available to them
- An easy way to request access to the app

- An easy way for the app to be installed or made available to the user
- (Possibly) an easy way for the app to be updated

So what's the difference between an app store and the old way? App stores are cool now!

As we already mentioned, the main advantage of an app store is that it's designed to be something that end users themselves see. (Though once they click on an app to request it, it's up to you to ensure that the app is able to be installed on their device.) Most corporate app stores can also be integrated into some kind of workflow, so if a user requests an app that's not available to them, an approval request could automatically be sent to their manager, licenses could be purchased, etc.

We're also starting to see app stores that cross platforms. HTML5 apps (whether internally hosted or SaaS) can be delivered to any device, as can Windows desktop applications that are coming from RDSH or VDI in the data center. Most corporate app stores can also deliver packaged Windows virtual apps (App-V, ThinApp, etc.) that will run on the client, and several newer ones can deliver native device apps to tablets and smart phones. Citrix Cloud Gateway Enterprise and the VMware Horizon app manager could certainly be called cross-platform app stores.

Integrating the data

So far we're part way to our goal. We can deliver different kinds of apps with varying degrees of success, and some aspects of user identity are still pretty hard to figure out. Fortunately, when it comes to data, we can have a bit more luck. We touched briefly on the importance of corporate data back in Chapter 9, and it's worth revisiting here as we try to hook everything together.

When it comes to data integration, the "data" we're talking about is files and folders. Sure, there's plenty of data locked up in corporate applications (databases, patient records, etc.), but that data is usually delivered as part of the application. So that's why we're just talking about files and folders here.

The easiest, most effective, and most user-friendly way to integrate data is to use some kind of file synchronization tool with support for plenty of native client platforms. This way your users end up with access to their My Documents folder no matter where they are. (Most choose to automatically sync the entire folder to laptops and to simply provide on-demand access to their files when connecting from tablets and smart phones.)

The most widely used example of this is Dropbox. While other file sync platforms continuously pop up, Dropbox has emerged as a favorite. If you're wondering why Dropbox is Number One, there's a great quote by Michael Wolfe in Quora about Dropbox:

> *Well, let's take a step back and think about the sync problem and what the ideal solution for it would do:*
> - *There would be a folder.*
> - *You'd put your stuff in it.*
> - *It would sync.*
>
> *They built that.*

He nailed it. Dropbox didn't try to solve the task management problem. (Every organization uses a different app for that.) They didn't try to solve the collaboration problem. (Again, there are a million other apps for that.) What Dropbox did build was a folder that syncs.

What's important to know from an IT perspective is that in today's world, your users need a way to access their files from any device, regardless of form factor or OS. If you want to let them use Dropbox (or if you want to buy the team version of Dropbox), that's great. You're done. But if you don't think that Dropbox is secure, you have to provide them with some other option that you are comfortable with. You can't just tell them not to use Dropbox because they're going to use it anyway and you'll never know about it.

If you decide that your data "solution" is going to be old-school SMB file shares that are only available when the user is connected to the VPN, that's not going to fly and your users will just use Dropbox.

On the other hand, if you say, "Don't use Dropbox because it's not secure. Instead use this. It works the same way and everything you do here is automatically backed up, encrypted, and made available to your colleagues. And our solution also has a Windows, Mac, Android, iOS, Blackberry, and web client, and it easily lets you share files with outside people." If you do that, then yes, of course your users will stop using Dropbox.

Fortunately, when it comes to file syncing, there are several enterprise-focused products to choose from. If you want to host everything yourself using your own servers (or servers from cloud providers you choose), you can use something like RES Software's HyperDrive. VMware is also getting close to releasing an offering that's currently code-named Octopus, and last year Citrix bought a company called ShareFile, which does the same thing. (And there are probably plenty more of these that we don't even know about.) From the user's perspective, these products provide functionality that's as good as Dropbox. And from IT's perspective, they're even better, with features like better enterprise integration, more security options, the ability to host as much data as you want, and specific control over the data storage location.)

If you don't want to host your file syncing solution yourself, there are a lot of SaaS-based Dropbox competitors out there, too. Maybe Dropbox isn't for you, but instead you could use Box, SugarSync, SkyDrive, or any of the other dozen offerings. Each of them focuses on a specific niche, so if you want to buy this as a cloud service but don't like Dropbox, there's probably something out there that would work for you.

Where Does This Leave Client Device Management?

Okay, so we've looked at integrating security, delivering multiple types of applications, and dealing with the user personalities and data. Now let's look at the client devices themselves.

No more need to manage

In the beginning of this book, we talked about how end-user desktops and the Windows OS that runs on them are closely intertwined. Because of this, we administrators have traditionally had to manage everything down there. (The Windows OS, patches, applications, hardware, devices—we had no choice!)

Hopefully after reading this far into the book you've realized that while we'll still have to deal with the Windows OS for a long time, we're trying to get to the point where we don't have to deal with Windows on the client device. If we can get there, it's only a small step toward our ultimate fantasy of not worrying about the client device at all. (If that ever comes true, we can let our users do whatever they want on their clients, since they can't negatively impact our ability to deliver their apps, data, and personal settings as a service.)

BYO

If we get so far as to not need to manage the client device, the next logical progression is to think, "Hey, if I'm letting my users do whatever they want on their client devices, why do they have to do it on my devices? Instead of giving them some crappy plastic corporate laptops, why not let each user choose whichever laptop makes him or her happy?"

And just like that, the seeds of the "bring your own computer" (BYOC) concept were sown. BYOC is the notion of end users "owning" their own laptops while IT resources (such as apps, data, and backup) are delivered as a service. The thinking is that as today's workforce becomes more comfortable with computers in general, your users will inevitably want to do things you don't want to support (like installing their own applications and storing personal data). Today's tech-savvy users also want some personal choice in which type of laptop they use. (Mac versus PC, full size and powerful versus ultra-small, etc.)

The concept of BYOC has been talked about for over a decade, but it was never a real option until recently, since there hadn't traditionally been a good way to cleanly separate "work stuff" from "personal stuff" on the same laptop. But now, thanks to everything we've been talking about in this book (client VMs, application streaming, seamless data center-hosted apps, etc.), it's actually quite simple for IT to provide their apps and desktops as a service and for users to "own" their own laptops.

We believe that the BYOC concept is brilliant, and it's something we feel the majority of users should be able to enjoy. But, of course, not everyone thinks like us! One of the objections we hear most often when we ask people about BYOC in their environment is that they would never allow corporate data on personal devices. (Or they say their company would never allow end users to bring in their own unmanaged laptops.)

Our next question to them is, "Do your users have admin rights on their laptops?"

At least 90% of people answer, "Yes."

"Well, my friend, if your users have admin rights on their laptops, then you're already doing BYOC!"

At this point, we usually hear protests in the form of, "Not true! The company owns the laptop."

But it doesn't matter. If a user has admin rights on the company laptop, that user "owns" the laptop. It doesn't matter what name is on the asset tag or who literally paid for it—if users can do whatever they want to a laptop, they own it.

That's a big misconception with the whole BYOC concept—some people think the "own" in BYOC refers to how the laptop was literally purchased. Wrong. The "own" in BYOC is about who "owns" the control of the laptop. Sure, some companies want to implement BYOC programs to save from having to select, buy, and manage the laptops (i.e., the program is a slick way to shift more expenses onto the workers), but the majority of companies that have implemented BYOC still buy the laptops for the users.

In practical terms, there are several ways the "own" can happen in BYOC:

- The employee owns the laptop. They literally bring in whatever they want.
- The employee owns the laptop. IT sets a minimum set of specifications the device must meet.

- The employee owns the laptop. IT specifies certain brands and models they will support.

- The company owns the laptop. Employees are given a stipend to buy whatever they want with the allotted amount. The employee can spend their own money above and beyond as they choose.

- The company owns the laptop. The employee has no choice about make or model, but the employee has admin rights and can install whatever he or she chooses.

Your company most likely falls into one of the categories above. (We'd argue that the last bullet is the way that laptops are managed in the majority of real-world companies anyway.) The important point is that the two types of ownership—who bought the laptop and who manages the laptop—are completely independent variables.

Regardless of the degree of BYOC in your company, if you just focus on delivering your applications and data as a service, it should be possible for your users to consume your applications alongside whatever they find and install on their own. (If you want to build a BYOC program, there's a lot more you have to deal with—HR policies, legal issues, how your firewalls and network access control works, etc. But that's a topic for a future book.) Our point here is to show you that if you deliver your apps and data as a service, you don't have to worry about the laptops.

One final note on users bringing their own devices: A lot of users are going to bring in iPads and then want to use their Windows desktop apps on their iPads. Fortunately, your RDSH and VDI desktops and applications will work fine on the iPad. The big downside is that the iPad doesn't work with a mouse. But that's not your fault. If you have desktop applications that require a proper keyboard and mouse, you can use RDSH and VDI to deliver them to the users no matter where they are. If you have a user who decides to connect from an iPad but doesn't like the experience, that's his fault, not yours. Tell him to get a device with a mouse and to stop complaining.

Are Mobile Devices a Template for the Future?

Android and iOS devices never had a traditional Windows desktop container to tie everything together, yet people seem to be getting along fine with them. Users are able to install and remove their own apps and can select among web, SaaS, and native choices. Companies are able to deliver services and apps while maintaining the control they need. And both sides are able to operate happily and independently of each other. We believe this is a template for what the future of corporate computing, desktops, and devices will look like.

To be clear, when we suggest you can look to iOS or Android for a glimpse of the future, we're talking in the context of what users control, what the companies control, and how everything is tied together. We don't want you to think, "Hey! Those devices don't have keyboards and mice, so they will never replace PCs." Remember that we previously said that believing Windows is dead or that the PC is dead does not mean the keyboard and mouse are dead. So when we look to iOS or Android for inspiration, we're talking about the computing model and the ecosystem—not the fact that the devices are keyboardless touch-based devices.

Let's take a closer look at the specifics of why we think today's "mobile" will be a good indication of the future.

App management

Today's mobile devices have app stores. Organizations can push apps to managed devices, and security settings can differ for each app. There are also Windows remoting clients for all of these mobile devices that allow them to access Windows desktop applications running in remote RDSH or VDI environments, and while the user experience isn't the best, it does show that it's possible to deliver old-school Windows applications to new-style devices.

We also have enough experience with delivering Windows applications to these new devices to know that if you lean on those old apps too heavily, your users will just stop using them and find their own native apps that do what they want. This has forced companies to step up and provide device-native apps, web apps, and SaaS apps in order to keep users happy. If it can happen for the mobile devices today, it can happen for all devices tomorrow.

Identity

Mobile devices handle identity in a pretty cool way. A user associates their device with their central identity (Apple ID, Google account, etc.) and then everything else—apps, settings, photos, high scores, data backup, etc.—are taken care of. The only real downside today is that the identities are tied to the platform providers. (If you want to use an iPhone, you must have an Apple ID, and an Android device requires a Google account.) Hopefully in the future we'll see some ability for identity providers other than the big platform providers. (Or maybe we'll see the ability for users to leverage their platform identities for corporate applications and data, too.)

We also need to see some evolution around how the platform identities are used for specific apps and websites. It would be great for your users to be able to log into a generic device with a single identity that you provide and to have that device spring to life with all their applications, settings, and data.

It's possible to use various software packages to enable Windows desktops to do this now, so when we look to the future, we expect that will continue (just in a more cross-platform way).

Data management

Data and file management on mobile devices is working great and a shining example of what's possible. Dropbox and the other services (both on-premises and hosted) do a wonderful job of providing access to users' files and folders. Many products even offer file caching for offline use with full encryption in case a device is lost.

Device management

One of the big differences between the Windows desktop world and the mobile device world is that mobile devices don't have to be managed like Windows desktops do. We discussed the reasons for this back in Chapter 7—Windows was designed twenty years ago, when any application was able to do whatever it wanted, while the mobile OSes were designed in the last five years and are very restrictive. This is why the mobile OSes are largely unaffected by the issues that plague Windows computers, such as viruses, malware, application issues, and crashes.

When Windows started to catch on in the business world, an entire desktop management industry sprung up just to handle these issues, with features such as software deployment, security policy enforcement, and configuration management. This kind of control was necessary, since Windows couldn't handle it on its own. Companies didn't love it, but they dealt with it.

In the past few years, when mobile devices became popular (read: once Apple released the iPhone), these same desktop management vendors took notice. Whether it was because they felt threatened or sensed a huge opportunity, they used their twenty years of desktop management knowledge to create software to manage the mobile devices. In an instant, the mobile device management (MDM) industry was born.

While customers loved MDM software—"Yay! We can control the devices just like we control the desktops"—the reality is that mobile devices didn't actually need the same kind of control that Windows desktops did. After all, mobile devices didn't allow multitasking, they could only run approved software, and they had twenty-plus years of experience factored into the secure design of their OS.

Nevertheless, the MDM industry pressed on and customers bought MDM software whose features read just like the features of the desktop management software from the prior decade. But the reality is that, in general, mobile devices don't need to be managed like desktop computers. They have inherently different architectures and needs.

Some vendors are going even crazier. The virtualization industry has attempted to solve this nonexistent device management problem with virtualization, using a complete mobile hypervisor to create separate VMs for work and personal environments on mobile devices. But since mobile applications are already isolated, creating a separate VM for security reasons is unnecessary. So while the pro-virtualization crowd was amazed (just like they were when VMware invented VDI), just like VDI, mobile hypervisors are a result of the same "we might as well virtualize it" attitude.

Fortunately, there's a better way to handle mobile devices via something called mobile application management (MAM). MAM software manages the applications on a device instead of trying to manage the device itself. For example, as an IT admin, you don't really care if the entire device has a passcode lock; you just want to make sure that the app that has access to your corporate data cannot be accessed without a passcode. You don't care if the entire device is encrypted; you just want to make sure the corporate data is encrypted. You don't need to remote-wipe the entire device if an employee quits; you just want to be able to wipe the corporate data and access.

The approach of only managing and protecting the corporate stuff while leaving the rest of the device alone is possible today, since mobile devices are based on operating systems that are decades newer than Windows. (This is not a dig on Windows—it's just the way it is.)

So what does this have to do with the future of devices? As we outlined back in Chapter 9, it is possible to deliver most Windows desktops applications as a service. In Chapter 10, we talked about how you can deliver native and web apps, and in this chapter, we've looked at how you can start to combine all these together. This all means you don't have to manage the client device, but instead you can manage the applications, settings, services, and data. If you need a real-world example, just look at the MAM vendors in the mobile device space today.

Don't Forget About Managing Windows

While it's fun to think about how great it would be if we could stop managing our users' devices, remember we discussed in Chapter 9 that we're going to have to manage the Windows OS as long as we have Windows desktop applications. (It's just that the copy of Windows that we're managing might be in a VM or a data center somewhere instead of on the user's client.)

We also discussed in Chapter 5 that as you're thinking about the various locations where Windows can run, you need to remember that running Windows the old-fashioned way—physically installed on a user's laptop or desktop—is a perfectly valid option in today's world. (And probably will be for some time.)

So in the context of how you're going to combine everything we've talked about so far—Windows desktops, Windows applications, native apps, web apps, data, settings, security, etc.—keep in mind that Windows is manageable, too. There are plenty of products that can do this, including Microsoft System Center Configuration Manager, Symantec's Altiris Client Management Suite, Tivoli's BigFix, LANDesk, Kace—the list goes on. Most of these products do the same types of things, including:

- Hardware and software inventory
- Asset and software license management
- Remote software distribution and delivery
- Patch management
- Imaging and migration

We opened this book by talking about the desktop life cycle: planning, provisioning, deployment, patching, maintaining, repeat. This life cycle can just as easily be used to describe the Windows desktop OS rather than the desktop hardware itself.

All these desktop and PC management tools work just as well on virtual desktops and virtual instances of Windows. After all, every feature in the above list describes the same features and capabilities you want for virtual desktop management, too.

Remember, Windows is old and needs to be managed. We talked at length about how you can pull some applications and data out, but when it comes to managing Windows, it shouldn't matter whether your instance is physical or virtual, running on the endpoint or running in the data center. The Windows management issues you need to deal with are the same either way, and you're going to have to deal with them as long as you have Windows applications.

Be Realistic with Today's Product Limitations

Calling this chapter "Putting it All Together" suggests that it's actually possible to put it all together. While there's a lot that can be done today, there are certain elements of this whole vision that just aren't ready yet. That doesn't mean that you shouldn't start thinking about everything now, but it does mean you probably won't be able to perfect everything in the next year or two.

For example, breaking up the Windows desktop and delivering it in little pieces is a new concept. Many of the technologies needed to make this happen work fine, but there's still a lot that doesn't work. (Some applications can't be remoted or virtualized, some peripherals don't work, etc.) Some people hear this and think, "Okay, forget it. We just won't do anything for a few years until everything is fully baked." Their thinking is that if they don't do anything now, they can just continue doing things the same way they've done them for the past fifteen years.

The problem with that approach is that the consumer-oriented SaaS apps and new devices available to users today are changing what users are able to do on their own. So you have to decide what you want to support—do you want to keep doing things the old way while leaving users to figure things out on their own with their iPads, or do you want to get in front of it and try to help them? (We swear that's not a leading question. Either answer is fine as long as you're confident.)

Equally frustrating is that fully embracing this new way of thinking is going to make you want to pull your hair out, at least in the short term. For example, we advocate that you deliver your business apps centrally while letting your users do all the personal things they need locally. But if you do that, do you really expect that users are going to switch back and forth between their remote and local desktops? That seems awkward.

You could instead deliver all your corporate applications from the data center via seamless windows, but then your users would have quirky anomalies like not being able to drag and drop files between local and remote applications. That's also awkward.

The only option that ensures a completely normal user experience is if you gave your users full control of their PC and if you delivered your corporate apps so that they ran locally. (In other words, the only way to guarantee a normal user experience is to keep doing things the same way you've been doing them for the past fifteen years.) But that means you'd have to support that entire instance of Windows and everything that goes along with it without the other benefits of desktop virtualization. So instead you can... You see? This process goes on and on!

The other big challenge to putting all this together is that the desktop computing environment is changing so fast. As soon as you get Windows 7 rolled out, your users will see Microsoft's huge Windows 8 campaign. As soon as you get your iOS and Android strategy worked out, all your favorite apps will start coming out for Windows 8 on ARM.

The bottom line is that you can't do everything at once, and your requirements are going to evolve as you're going along. While it might make for good job security, it's certainly not going to make your life easier.

Specific Action Items You Can Do Now

We've talked about a lot of theory, strategy, and long-term stuff in this book. And even though our purpose is to explain why

VDI hasn't taken over the world and what the alternative desktops will look like, we understand that a lot of people reading this book are hoping to get specific ideas for what can be done today.

So we'll close out this "putting it all together" chapter with a list of specific things we would do today if we were in charge of the IT department for an existing company filled with lots of traditional desktop and laptop users. These items are not in any specific order, and some may not even apply to your environment, since every situation is different. But if we were in charge, it would go down like this:

Implement some kind of user workspace management

You're probably aware that Windows roaming profiles have some serious limitations, including the fact that you can't share profiles between different versions of Windows, profiles aren't designed for a single user to be logged into multiple Windows desktops at the same time, and there's a lot of stuff that users can change and install that just isn't saved in the profile folder.

We mentioned several vendors with products in this space, including AppSense, RES Software, triCerat, Immidio, and Scense, as well as the big desktop virtualization vendors Citrix, VMware, and Quest. (Each vendor has their own name for these products, including "user workspace management," "user personality management," or simply "user virtualization.") Call them what you will—what's important is that you use one of them. (Any one!)

If it were up to us, we'd implement one of these user workspace things in your existing physical Windows desktop environment. That way your new tool can start collecting data and settings from your existing users and can then be used to build their environment as they log into other types of desktops (VDI, RDSH, etc.).

Once you've pulled that user configuration out of Windows, you ought to be able to apply it to other environments as the personalization vendors extend their products. (Although, if not, you'll eventually need to separate out the user configuration just to make your Windows environment work, so you might as well get started with that on your existing physical desktops before you try to start virtualizing them.)

Start using app virtualization

The other big thing we'd do is to start using app virtualization for as many of your Windows desktop applications as feasible. (We're talking about Microsoft App-V, VMware ThinApp, Symantec Workspace Virtualization, Numecent, Spoon, InstallFree, etc.)

Our thinking is that you have all these Windows desktop apps that you have to support (both for your virtual and physical desktops), so why not make it easier for yourself and package as many of them as you can? Every app you package and can deliver virtually is one more app you don't have to manually install. Then once they're packaged, it's easy to deploy that same package to an instance of Windows. It doesn't matter if it's physical, VDI, a client VM, or an RDSH session.

A lot of people get hung up on the decision about which app virtualization platform they should use. They always try to find which one's "best" by looking at what percentage of apps it can package. Our belief is that doesn't really matter. If it can't do 100% (none can), that means you'll still have to support some tradition-al (nonpackaged) apps. And as long as you're supporting some of each, it doesn't really matter if the ratio is 95/5, 90/10, or even 70/30. To be honest, most people just package the ones that have complicated or conflicting installs and the super-easy ones. They end up with about 50% of their Windows desktop applications packaged as virtual apps. And while 50% means they're still deal-ing with a lot of traditional desktop apps, the total number is 50% fewer than if they weren't using app virtualization at all.

(By the way, save yourself the trouble and don't try to virtu-alize Microsoft Office—just build it into the base Windows image. Packaging Office just leads to a lot of headaches around how it interacts with other app packages, so most people just build it into their base image and consider it part of the operating system.)

Move as many Windows desktop apps into the data center as possible

One of the simplest things you can do to change the amount of end-user support you have to provide at the desktop level is to start pulling Windows desktop applications off of the users' laptops and desktops. The easiest way to do this is to install the apps onto an RDSH (or the related Citrix XenApp or Quest vWorkspace) server and then provide seamless remoting access to the Windows application directly.

Of course doing so means that users can only use the application when they're connected to the network, and the application must be capable of being run out of a remote data center. You also need to ensure that the remote application won't need any integration with local applications beyond simple copying and pasting. (For example, if your users need to drag and drop items from their local desktop to the remote app, that's not going to work.)

But if you can afford it and your apps support it, moving as many apps to RDSH or VDI servers in your data center will make your client support much easier.

Re-examine your firewalls

Most organizations have a few extra classifications for their network beyond the simple "internal" and "external." They want to ensure that the data center is more secure than the user network, the user network is more secure than the guest network, and the guest network is more secure than the Internet. Still, there are others who are very blind in their approach, protecting only the perimeter and giving carte blanche access to anything inside the firewall, including full network access to devices in the data center. The second approach is somewhat lazy (or "easy," depending on how you see it), and it leads to an environment where more and more users bring unmanaged devices into the workplace. Seriously, would you let just anyone hook up a rooted (vulnerable) Android device in your data center? Heck no!

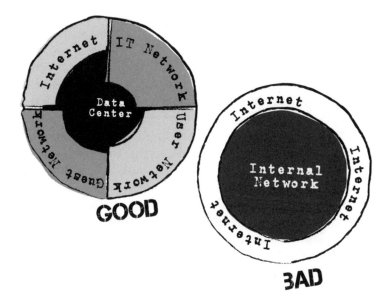

Well-planned organizations elevate the security around the apps, data, and services that run in the data center, and these organizations are already a step ahead of the rest as they begin allowing certain devices on the network. At the very least, it means that an unmanaged device connected outside the data center doesn't have full network access to the data center. It doesn't stop someone from plugging a WiFi access point into a user land network cable, but it does prevent that device from accessing everything.

Companies that go this route can further segment their network to accommodate other devices or users. The drawing above has separate network security levels for IT personnel, guests (including contractors), and normal users on traditional desktops. The whole point of this is to protect the data center network from less-secure networks outside.

Extreme cases could treat anything outside the data center as 100% insecure (Internet-level insecurity), which is perhaps too restrictive to make a mixed-device use case practical. The government goes beyond this, with racks and even servers having their own firewalls. We're not saying that you need to go to those extremes, but what we are saying is that in order to responsibly accommodate these new, unmanaged devices, you'll need to do something beyond what was common IT practice ten years ago.

But even going to these lengths won't be enough if you leave your wireless network wide open, allow unsanctioned wireless networks, or allow just anyone to plug into non-guest networks. Wireless intrusion prevention systems can be used to prevent rogue wireless networks, and network management solutions can prevent bridging events like ones that could be caused by tethering a mobile phone to a laptop connected to the corporate network. On more secure networks, things like Network Level Authentication are also effective at restricting access to those that need it.

How you configure your network depends on what you're trying to achieve, but there is no one-size-fits-all solution. The best-laid plans amount to ones with varying levels of security and flexibility, and these are all based on the demands of the users, applications, and services. So, if you haven't already, divide up your network security. Allow users to connect wireless devices, but make sure they connect to a network that is somehow isolated from the important networks. Not only does that limit your WiFi attack surface, but it also sets you up for the next topic: embracing BYO.

Embrace the BYO concept

We discussed the concept of BYOC earlier in this chapter. (Remember the "C" stands for computer. There's a related concept called BYOD, where the "D" stands for "device," like a smart phone or tablet.) The main thing behind BYO is that you need to embrace it, because users are going to start working from their own devices whether you like it or not. So if you deliver your Windows desktop applications as a service and all your users really need on their device is a copy of Office and a browser, you can probably start letting users bring in their own computers. If it makes them happy and you don't have to manage the device, what do you care?

Hosted email (or open email)

There are so many awesome consumer-oriented products out there that plug into existing email systems. (We're talking contact management, social apps, CRM-like tracking apps, etc.) But if your email system is restrictive and blocks POP or IMAP access, your users are just going to forward all their email to Gmail. (It's ironic! You restrict everything in the name of security, but you end up with an environment that's not secure because everything was too hard for the users to access so they just used whatever they found on their own.)

Data and file sync

We talked about this earlier in the chapter. When we're looking at the big picture of what actions we'd take today if we were in charge of a company's desktops and applications, we'd make sure that every employee in that company had a Dropbox-like file syncing and backup tool.

Some people feel like IT shouldn't try to compete against these consumer services—that we'll always be chasing whatever the latest fad is and we'll never be able to offer anything as good. While that could certainly be true in some cases, come on—in this case we're just talking about data. Users want their files wherever they are, and they want them to live locally on their devices and to always be in sync. There are plenty of products that do that today. And just like with the email servers, if you don't give users easy ways to replicate and share their files, they're just going to figure out a way to do it anyway.

Can We Put the Future Together Today?

Based on everything we discussed in this chapter and the specific steps you can take today, are we in the position to deliver the future desktop today? For most of us, the answer is no. We just have too many Windows desktop applications to deal with. And even if we can deliver them remotely to iPads and other unknown devices, the experience isn't perfect. Combine that with the varying levels of product maturity and the quickly evolving device landscape, and there's suddenly a lot of motivation to simply move your existing Windows to VDI in order to ride out the storm. (VDI is a great stopgap for people who don't know what to do. And if it gives you another few years of Windows desktops as usual, all the better!)

Rather than trying to figure out if you can do everything today, just focus on one thing at a time. All we ask is that you keep these truths in mind:

- Windows desktop applications will be around for a long time.
- The desktop can be broken down into its core parts.
- Users will have lots of different devices, all with different form factors and OSes.
- If you tell users they can't do something, they'll probably do it anyway.
- Mixing Windows desktop applications with new native applications will be clunky at best, but you still have to deal with it.

So how will all this coalesce into the desktop of the future? Let's find out.

Chapter 12

The Future of the Desktop

I<small>T'S HUMAN NATURE TO ENVISION THE FUTURE</small> only in terms of the present. Remember all the iPhone predictions from Apple fans that were published before it was first announced in 2007? They all looked like iPods or Nokia smart phones. Henry Ford was famously quoted as saying, "If I had asked people what they wanted, they would have said, 'a faster horse.'" This is why when you ask people to predict the future of the desktop, they describe things like web-based browser desktops that still have icons and wallpapers and Start buttons.

But after reading this entire book, you now understand that the desktop of the future isn't going to look like a Windows desktop in a browser. You know the desktop is a concept, not a concrete thing. So for us to answer the question, "What will the future desktop look like?" we have to figure out which desktop the person asking the question is talking about. Are they asking about the future of Windows or the future of the PC? Maybe they're asking about the future of devices with keyboards and mice? Or perhaps they want to know about the future of end-user computing in general?

Since it's possible that you'll run into people asking any of these questions, let's take a look at each of them one by one.

The Future of Windows

We've spent a good portion of this book discussing the future of the Windows OS and Windows applications. So if anyone ever asks you about the future of Windows, just give them your copy of this book. (Actually on second thought, tell them to buy their own!) Just keep in mind when discussing the future of Windows that there are actually two questions to answer:

- How will we deliver existing legacy Windows desktop applications?
- What will the Windows apps of the future look like?

Let's take a look at each of these.

The future of legacy Windows desktop applications

We recognize that it can be a bit reckless to throw around words like "legacy" to describe the millions of existing Windows desktops applications that are out there. We certainly don't want to offend anyone, especially those who are in the midst of developing, buying, and deploying these kinds of Windows applications. That said, Microsoft has made it clear with the Windows 8 Metro, Windows Store, and WinRT-based apps that the Windows native applications of the past twenty years are legacy.

That said, we all know that these legacy Windows desktop applications will continue to be developed, and we're sure that they will continue to be used for decades to come. Notwithstanding everything we've said in this book so far, it's our belief that legacy Windows desktop applications will make a slow, yet inevitable, migration to the data center.

This move to the data center will take decades, and in fact, we don't advocate that you run out and try to move all your existing Windows desktop applications to the data center anytime soon. As we said previously, there are some great use cases for putting Windows desktop applications in the data center, but running them locally on client laptops and desktops is just too cheap, easy, and compelling today. So right now we only want to move them into the data center when it makes sense.

Over time, however, we'll see that legacy Windows desktop applications make up a smaller and smaller portion of our overall application set. This trend is visible already. Ten years ago, most of us had 100% Windows apps. Five years ago, we might have had an 80/20 Windows-to-web apps split. Now, it might be 50/50. If you play that out a few years, you'll see that we'll eventually get to the point where we only have a small handful of legacy Windows desktop applications. At that point, we'll have to ask ourselves, "Do we really want to support Windows and everything that goes with it on every client just to make a few apps work?"

If you're dreading this inevitability, it's quite possible it won't be as bad as you think. For example, at BriForum Chicago 2010 (our own desktop virtualization conference), Atlantis Computing founder Chetan Ventakesh gave a brilliant talk where he explained why our Windows desktops and legacy applications are destined for the data center.

Chetan explained that Moore's Law is worthless when it comes to distributed desktop computing. Sure, it's great that we can get more processing for our money each year, but desktop computers are more or less stuck at the same price points they've been at for the past decade, and doubling the processing of a desktop doesn't change the computing model at all.

In the data center, however, we can apply this concept of "dematerialization," meaning physical objects are transformed into an abstract concept. Dematerialization of the desktop provides the liquidity whereby a desktop doesn't have to run within the boundaries of a single box. He's not talking about flowing an entire monolithic desktop VM from one server host to another. Rather, Chetan believes we'll be able to break up the memory, disk, data, CPU, and personalization so that each can run in the most performant and appropriate way.

Chetan proposed that the Windows desktop will grow to fill the boundaries of the data center, rather than the boundaries of a single computer. For example, by 2015:

- The rack is the new computer
- 10 Gigabit Ethernet is the new bus
- The hypervisor is the new kernel
- The software mainframe is the new OS

In order to get this type of liquidity, the desktop can't run on a client—it's got to run in a data center. While the data center is an expensive and complex place to run Windows desktop applications today, Moore's law is making it more attractive every year. In 2010, we could only run 70 desktop VMs per physical server, which means we could fit 1,120 desktops in a rack. In 2012, we can run 150 desktops per server, or 2,400 in a single rack. Playing that forward, we'll be able to run 4,800 desktops in a rack by 2014, and 9,600 by 2016. Throughout that whole process, our per-desktop VM hardware cost drops from $400 to $150.

As desktop VM density increases, we'll see the boundaries of a VM break down. We already have some pretty amazing technologies for VMs in the data center, like Cisco UCS, block-level single-instance storage, memory-based disk caching, and the ability to boot live VMs with no storage. IOPS, once the killer of VDI, are now manageable. In the meantime, the amount of IOPS and CPU that a given version of Windows needs remains constant even as hardware gets faster. (Of course, Microsoft's desire to support that given version does not, so we'll probably still see hardware requirements inflate for new Windows versions over the years. But if you're just using Windows in the data center for legacy applications, you ought to be able to deliver them more cheaply each year.)

All these technological advancements mean that running Windows on VDI in the data center will be able to deliver a better experience than what's possible when running Windows on a client. In his talk, Chetan said, "Imagine that everything is instant. Apps open instantly. Docs open instantly. Everything is snappy and perfect. That's the experience that a dematerialized desktop running in a data center can deliver." At that point, the users can vote with their feet, so to speak. Combine that with the security, reliability, and falling costs, and Chetan believes that VDI is a no-brainer for the majority of use cases for Windows desktop applications.

Chetan closed his talk with this final thought: VDI is not just the sum composite of knee-jerk reactions to PC management, but rather it's a long-term transformational vector—the natural evolution of computing, and something that can't be ignored.

Windows applications without Windows?

One axiom we've repeated throughout this book is that having even one single Windows application requires that we have Windows running somewhere. Some people wonder if that's actually true. They point out the open source project called Wine that attempts to re-create the Windows APIs and kernel calls in a software layer that can run on non-Windows operating systems. Wine is pretty amazing—you can literally run Windows EXEs on Mac or Linux OSes. The problem is that because Wine is reverse-engineered, it's always a few years behind in terms of what applications work. (At the time of this writing, Office 2010 doesn't yet work with Wine, and even Office 2007 has some major issues.) Because of this it's been easy to brush off Wine as a fun experiment, but not something that enterprises can trust.

Looking ahead, however, we have to wonder if that might change? If you believe that the biggest headaches in the future will be with legacy Windows desktop applications that can't be updated, you've got to think that at some point Wine will catch up. Sure, there are problems with Microsoft Office, but that's a huge suite, and there already are office suites for every platform—desktop users in the future aren't going to care about getting Microsoft Office from a Windows VM on their MacBook. So if the big concern is getting all these old proprietary Windows applications to run in the future, maybe Wine will work well.

On the other hand, running Wine still requires a full traditional OS. So if you use Wine to take Windows out of the picture, what do you really gain by replacing it with Mac or Linux? Are the Windows licenses that big of a deal?

Windows apps via HTML5?

Another concept we've covered quite a bit in this book is that it's possible to deliver Windows applications to users via HTML5. We focused on the various HTML5 clients for standard Windows applications running in the data center—things like VMware AppBlast or Ericom AccessNow. But there's another possibility. Companies like Framehawk are building solutions that let admins create HTML-based front ends for existing Windows desktop applications. The final result is apps that look and feel like native HTML5 apps, instead of the HTML5 Windows remoting clients that give users Windows-looking apps inside a browser.

Is this the way the last few Windows apps will be delivered from the data center in ten or twenty years? Perhaps.

Will Windows layering ever take off?

Throughout this book we've also touched a bit on a concept called "layering." Layering is the idea that you can slice Windows up into individual layers that are managed independently. You might have one layer for the base OS, another for corporate applications, and a third for user-installed applications.

Layering is not a product from a specific vendor. Instead it's more of a feature of desktop virtualization products or the description of what happens when you combine OS image management, application virtualization, and user personalization products.

The reason we mention layering in our discussion of the future is because layering is a hot topic right now. People initially believed layering would be necessary for VDI since they assumed that VDI could only work when many users shared a single master disk. (In those cases layering was thought to be the silver bullet that enabled users to have custom desktops based on a that common image.)

But advances in storage technologies have addressed the performance issues we initially thought only layering could solve. So now the conversation about layering has shifted to focus on leveraging it as a way to manage Windows desktops.

For example, some view layering as an application management solution. If you build a layer around each application, you can instantly enable and disable access to individual applications by turning a particular layer on or off. Another use is to support user-installed applications (UIAs)—the idea that users can install whatever they want into their own layer that is isolated from the base OS, (meaning IT can still refresh or patch the base layer without affecting the applications that the user has installed).

At the time of this writing, we don't know how this layering technology will fare and where exactly it will be the most popular. We know that the Windows OS and Windows desktop applications must be managed, and if doing so via layering makes more sense in virtual environments than traditional desktop management tools, that sounds great to us.

On the other hand, using layering strictly for user personality doesn't make as much sense to us. We spent this whole book writing about how users want their environment to work across platforms, so building up all these Windows-specific personality layers doesn't seem like it has much potential outside of Windows. We rather prefer the idea of creating the user personality as a separate thing that could ultimately be transferred across operating environments and devices.

The Future of the PC

The main shift of the PC over the past decade has been that ten years ago, the PC was the center of a user's world. It was the master copy that held the user's apps, data, and settings. It was everything. But nowadays, the PC is evolving to become just one of many consumption devices—in this case, in the form factor that allows for multiple displays and that has a keyboard and mouse.

This evolution wasn't based on any grand plan; rather, it was borne from necessity. Back when it was common for users to have one (and only one) computer, it was fine for that to be the master storage location for everything. But as we discussed in Chapter 8, smart phones, tablets, and Internet-based syncing means that the PC is no longer the linchpin that held the master copies of everything.

Does this mean the PC died? Of course not. Sure, the role changed. Now, instead of using a PC because we have to, we only use a PC when we want a full keyboard or multiple huge displays.

This evolution will continue. PCs (as compared to tablets, smart phones, or thin clients) have certain characteristics that will still have value in the next decade—they can support multiple displays and run many applications can run at the same time. They provide huge amounts of processing power locally. They have full-size keyboards that enable people to type at hundreds of words per minute and they have precision mice and pointing devices. And of course in the Ultrabook form factor, PCs enable all of these capabilities to be packed up and taken anywhere.

So it's true that the PC will relinquish its position as the center of a user's universe, but it's not going anywhere anytime soon.

The Future of Devices with Keyboards and Mice

Perhaps this goes without saying, based on what we just covered with our thoughts about the future of the PC, but we don't believe devices with keyboards or mice are going away anytime soon, either. There are some who believe that speech recognition will replace keyboards, but we just don't see it. Have you ever tried to dictate a document instead of typing it? It doesn't work for most people. This has nothing to do with the quality of the speech recognition programs. The problem with dictation is that speech comes from a different area of your brain. Speech is very linear, where typing allows you to mentally jump around and visually construct sentences.

Even if you were good enough to speak your way through your typing, how's that going to work when other people are around? It's bad enough that we have to listen to everyone's phone calls near us—now we have to listen to their typing, too? No thanks!

Finally, even though humans are not good at multitasking, most of us type and take notes while we're on the phone. How would that work if we have to talk to our computers?

We believe that there is a place for speaking to your devices. (Asking your phone a question while you're driving is brilliant.) But just like tablets didn't replace PCs, speaking to your computer isn't going to replace a keyboard.

The Future of End-User Computing

Everything we've discussed so far in this entire book—the applications, the data, and the devices—could broadly be grouped into something called "end-user computing." By now you ought to be able to see how it's all going to come together.

Users will seek out applications. They'll want to use them via multiple devices with multiple form factors. The applications will increasingly store their configuration and data in ways that disambiguate them from their devices. (Start the email on the phone, finish it on the laptop.) Cloud-based storage of everything will become ubiquitous, regardless of whether it's public or private, user-based or company-based. All the while, IT will continue to lose control over what devices users can use and how they can access data. Whether the user selects and owns a device or the company does won't matter. IT will control access to corporate apps and corporate data, but beyond that, the users are on their own.

The desktop of tomorrow won't run Windows. But it also won't run the Mac OS. Or iOS. Or Android. The desktop of tomorrow is not a Chromebook or based on a browser. The desktop of the future is whatever device the user has in his or her hands at any moment. It will have the user's applications, data, settings, and personality. It's nowhere and everywhere at once.

And it's going to be here long before Windows is dead. So get on it!

—Brian, Gabe, & Jack. March 2012

Chapter 13

The Unified Cloud

This chapter was written by Rick German, CEO of Stoneware. It was placed here because they bought this book to give to you.

So ARE BRIAN, GABE, AND JACK RIGHT? Is VDI more hype than reality? I believe, like they do, that VDI does have certain cases where it fits well. I was recently at VMworld, and ran into a few people where VDI met their specific needs.

One example that comes to mind was a customer who only wanted his developers to connect via VDI to a development environment. It was unique in that they were not able to move code out of that environment. VDI worked great for him in that niche. His users were given an image that contained all the tools needed. There was no need to manage a large set of disparate applications. Since everything was being done on the internal network, there were fewer concerns about network bandwidth and the end user experience.

The reality is that most end users do not fit so nicely into that niche. They have a wide-ranging variety of applications, they connect from multiple locations, and they use multiple devices. They just want a simple way to access their "stuff" from anywhere.

At VMWorld, I met person after person who had started down the VDI path, only to come to the realization that it wasn't going to meet the needs of their end users. There is a new world of end user computing, and VDI isn't going to cut it for the majority of users.

Where do we go from here? Do we wait for the desktop of the future to arrive or do we stitch together disparate products in an attempt to meet the demands of our end users? We believe that with the arrival of HTML5, CSS3, SSL and other web technologies the future is here today.

Stepping-Stone to the Future

Just as Brian mentioned, legacy Windows applications are going to be around for a long time. The trend is toward web-based applications but any IT delivery solution you use today will need to deliver Windows applications. Industries have invested significant time and money into these solutions, and in many cases, there just aren't good web alternatives available. Throw in the fact that most people are comfortable using Windows and you see why it will be around for a while.

But that doesn't mean that people are tied to a Windows desktop. IT is not about the desktop interface. It is all about the applications, files and reports end users need to get their jobs done, collaborate and share with colleagues, family and friends. The iPad is a great example of a new, simple, easy-to-use interface that people choose to use in addition to Windows. It's all about the resources. IT must deliver those resources quickly, easily and securely, plain and simple. We believe the right way to deliver those resources is through the web.

As web technologies mature, more and more options are possible. HTML5 and CSS3 are allowing things to be done via the web that were not possible just a couple of years ago. That's the beauty of technology. There are so many smart people coming up with a better "virtual" mousetrap.

What about the device? Does it really matter in the new cloud-based world or is a browser-based device all we need? Again, the iPad is the perfect example that we care deeply about what device we use. It is the poster child for consumerization and has changed the balance of power between IT and end users.

However, not all devices are equal and there should be a way to allow cloud services to take advantage of unique capabilities of particular devices. If you have a laptop that has the latest processor, you have a discrete graphics card, and a fast wired connection, you should get a better experience than the guy next to you who is attempting to access those same resources on a device with a 4 inch screen, over 3G. So how do you differentiate the end user experience, when the cloud today goes to the lowest common denominator?

Obviously Stoneware is sponsoring this chapter because we have a solution that meets the criteria of being secure, able to access files, applications and reports, and also comprehends the unique capabilities of devices, all delivered through web technologies. This solution is called webNetwork. Recently Stoneware was acquired by Lenovo. Lenovo's version of webNetwork is called Secure Cloud Access or SCA.

The Unified Cloud

webNetwork/SCA is a software solution installed in your datacenter that allows you to create a Unified Cloud for your organization. A Unified Cloud delivers resources from the private data center (like a web-based time card, or a vacation scheduler), resources from the public cloud (like Gmail, Zoho, or Salesforce.com), and also the resources available on your device (like Excel). These resources are presented to the user through a unified HTML5 webDesktop that provides a simple, consistent user experience through a single password.

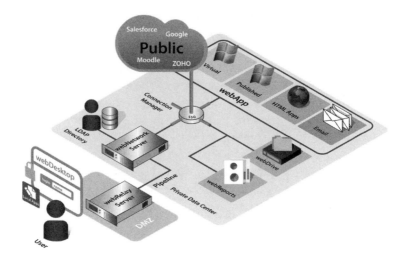

webNetwork/SCA sits on two servers, one in the DMZ, and another inside your data center. When a user logs into the secure webDesktop, their credentials are encrypted and sent to the data center and authenticated against a LDAP compliant directory. Once authenticated, the user is then given access to assets through the webDesktop that are appropriate based on their permissions. For example, if I am a junior level analyst, I might just get my time-card, and a couple of applications that I use in my job, but if I am the CEO, I get access to all the company reports and applications that I need to make sure the company is running smoothly.

Because the solution comprehends the device, we are also able to use and if needed send the appropriate resources to the device. Just because it is technically possible to send a terminal server version of Excel to a phone doesn't mean it is a good idea. In such a case, we set up a decision tree that allows you to open a spreadsheet that is appropriate for your device (like Office2HD), or signs you into a web service, like Google Docs, or Zoho, for you to complete your task.

This flexibility is one of the reasons why we believe the Unified Cloud delivers on the promises of VDI, without the drawbacks and at a fraction of the cost. End users access the "stuff" they need with one password, one interface, from anywhere on any device without the need for a VPN.

At the beginning of this book, Brian mentioned several promises that VDI said it would deliver, and the next chapter examined whether those were met. We would like to take those same promises, and show you how webNetwork/SCA fulfills them.

The Unified Cloud Delivers What VDI Promised

1. Saves Money

For most customers that have purchased and deployed Stoneware's webNetwork/SCA, cost was a major factor in the decision making process. The investment required for VDI in additional data center servers, equipment and training is simply too expensive.

webNetwork/SCA allows customers to minimize their data center investment while delivering a broad range of application and data delivery options for their end users. webNetwork/SCA accomplishes this by leveraging its unique "Intelligent Application Delivery".

Intelligent Application Delivery allows the cloud to dynamically determine, at runtime, when an application should be delivered locally, from the private data center, or out of the public cloud. By utilizing this technology, IT can make situational decisions that will impact both the cost of delivering an application as well as the overall end user experience. For example, Microsoft Office can be delivered by IT in many different ways; locally, virtualized, published, and web hosted (i.e. - Office 365). Each method has a different cost structure in backend resources and licensing. Using webNetwork/SCA, IT can determine the optimal delivery method at runtime. For some end users, editing a spreadsheet hosted in the data center with a local copy of Excel is the best and most cost effective solution. For others accessing the cloud from a tablet, a remotely published version of Excel may be a better solution.

The main point is that IT can setup the rules and therefore control the cost of delivering applications and data to their end users. The flexibility of webNetwork/SCA's technology enables IT to control costs while creating a single, Unified Cloud platform.

2. Provides Better Security

One of the strongest arguments for VDI is security. Both the applications and data reside in the data center under the control of IT where users never interact directly with the application or data. However, this may be a false sense of security. Ask any manager or executive that has a VDI solution at their disposal whether all of their spreadsheets, mail, presentations, and documents are secure back in the data center. You might be surprised to find out that almost all continue to use their local device (e.g. – tablet, notebook, laptop, etc.) to create, edit, and maintain certain corporate data. They all claim a variety of excuses: "I will be on a plane and want to work", "I could not connect to the network", "I am at a retreat", "My machine is not configured correctly", etc. The reality is that IT is "jail broken".

Users are accessing and working with data on their own terms. Security will have to accommodate the mode in which users want to interact with the either the data or the application.

webNetwork/SCA's approach is to match the security with the service being accessed through the Unified Cloud. With webNetwork/SCA, a user accessing a patient record system may need to do it through publishing technology, much like VDI where both the data and application are secured in the data center. However, the same user accessing a presentation or word processing document can edit it directly from their notebook or tablet device using the application of their choice. Stoneware believes that this approach will allow IT to appropriately control security and provide a better end user experience.

3. Users Can Work Anywhere, from Any Devic

With each passing day, the market continues wards a consumerized computing model. For many _ _ _, _ _ _, difficult to define where their work life ends and their personal life begins. Therefore IT, software vendors and hardware manufacturers should expect users to want a device serve both their personal and work related computing needs. In fact, organizations that fail to recognize this do so at their own peril.

Stoneware's webNetwork/SCA was designed with the understanding that users want access from anywhere using most any device. The decision by Stoneware to present cloud applications and services through a common HTML5 webDesktop meant that the solution could easily transition between a wide range of devices. At Lenovo this is the "Four Panes of Glass" strategy that targets smartphones, notebooks, tablets and TVs for services. With just an Internet connection, users can access their applications, files and data from any device that has a web browser.

The browser becomes the execution environment for the webNetwork/SCA Unified Cloud. The browser is ubiquitous; enabling users the freedom to access work related resources from anywhere. This strategy is important because an increasingly fluid workforce finds itself accessing cloud resources from a host of consumerized devices.

4. Provides a Good End User Experience

As the Brian explains in earlier chapters, the remote desktop experience for end users has gotten progressively better over the last five years. Remote protocols have gotten faster, more feature-rich and efficient. However a funny thing happened while developers were working to perfect deficiencies of remote control protocols. The market shifted with the introduction of a new breed of touch devices like smartphones and tablets, which exposed the weakness of the "Windows Everywhere" strategy.

We learned is that users prefer an experience that matches the device. If the device supports touch, then users wants a touch experience. A remote Windows interface built with small icons, tiny buttons, and difficult to click menu options is a recipe for frustrated users. Understanding this, Stoneware's Universal web-Desktop dynamically adapts to the device accessing the cloud. The Universal web desktop detects the type of device (i.e. – touch vs. pointer) as well as the size of the screen. Menus, tiles, graphics, and icons automatically adapt to create an experience for the end user that makes navigating and locating cloud services with web-Network/SCA easy and hassle-free.

In addition to adapting the desktop interface to the device, users want to interact with the data in a way that is more native to the device. Many users have a better experience interacting with their data using one of the many simple, single-purpose applications available at an application store. webNetwork/SCA's integrated private cloud storage technology, webDrive, allows the end user to easily interact with their corporate data (i.e. – spreadsheets, documents, and presentations) on the network using local, native applications. In almost all cases, this creates a better experience for the tablet and smartphone user.

5. Environmentally Friendly

We agree with Brian and his arguments that VDI is probably not going to any more environmentally friendly than the traditional model. Stoneware believes the right answer here is to use the correct power schemes available on each device. One of the features of webNetwork/SCA is called webManage. Through webManage you'll be able to see and set power profiles for supported devices.

6. Client Devices Last Longer

Because webNetwork/SCA is a web-based solution, a device with an internet connection and a browser is all that is needed to access your files, applications and data.

For most customers this translates to an increase in the desktop refresh rate. Many of our customers have moved from a three year hardware refresh rate to a five year refresh rate.

7. Reduced Downtime Due to Hardware Failure

One of the benefits of cloud, HTML5, and other web technologies is ready access from a wide range of devices. Building webNetwork/SCA on a foundation of web technologies means that the cloud and its services are accessible anytime from almost any device that the user has in hand.

Users experiencing hardware failure on their primary computing device can easily grab or borrow another notebook, tablet, or smartphone and continue accessing their files, data and applications from the Unified Cloud. No provisioning or re-imaging are necessary. By relying on a simple web browser, IT organizations easily reduce end user related downtime by allowing a broader range of devices to access corporate IT applications and services.

8. Better Disaster Recovery and Business Continuity

There is no doubt the VDI strategy of all desktops running back in the data center has a compelling business continuity story. However, building a VDI deployment for disaster recovery significantly increases the cost of an already expensive backend solution. Doubling the backend server and disk infrastructure for VDI at an off-site location is often financially out of reach for most commercial and public organizations.

By focusing on application delivery and not disk images, webNetwork/SCA has a significantly smaller data center footprint that can be mirrored to off-site locations at relatively minimum cost. Session-level clustering technology contained within webNetwork/SCA means that a user can seamlessly switch between severs located in separate data centers without losing their session or their work.

9. Easier Image Management

VDI provides easier image management than a traditional standalone PC environment. Images are transferred over high-speed data center network. Images are stored and maintained on large storage networks. Images can be updated at the click of a button – sounds great. It sounds great until one realizes that IT's real task is delivering an application or service and not an image. End users are not looking to access a remote desktop; they are trying to access business applications.

Focusing on the delivery of applications means that webNetwork/SCA is not trapped by the concept of "image management." In fact, webNetwork/SCA does not have any of the requirements that typically go with a VDI solution. Instead, webNetwork/SCA administrators focus on configuring a set of applications and services in the cloud.

The webNetwork/SCA Unified Cloud platform supports a wide variety of applications including internal web, public web, published Windows, virtualized Windows, and local device applications. Because the solution does no attempt to be a remote desktop image, the backend server and storage costs are dramatically reduced. This greatly simplifies the management and delivery of services.

10. Simpler Provisioning

Because VDI is grounded in a desktop image, provisioning that image with applications, updates, and patches is a time consuming, labor intensive process. A web approach without the provisioning of desktops means that the IT organization can focus on providing cloud applications and services. webNetwork/SCA integrates with an organization's directory service (e.g. – Active Directory). Deployment of applications and services in the cloud can be assigned directly to a user, group, or organizational unit. With tight directory service integration, much of the daily provisioning of applications and services can be handed over to help desk personnel. When a network user is assigned to a specific group or organization, they can immediately inherit the applications and services from the webNetwork/SCA Unified Cloud.

11. Better User Isolation

Unlike VDI, at Stoneware our goal is not to isolate the desktop from the device. We find that users like the experience of running a local operating system on the device and would most often choose to do their daily work directly on the device.

By using their own devices running a local operating system, users are inherently isolated from the slow downs and disadvantages of server based computing.

12. More Consistent Performance

Survey your users and they will tell you eight out of ten times that the best performance and experience is typically when application executes directly from their personal device. While VDI has the potential to deliver better performance, there are many external factors that can impact the end user experience. Factors such as available network bandwidth, backend server CPU load, etc. can alter the experience for the end user.

Stoneware, in combination with Lenovo and the Cloud Ready Client, utilizes Intelligent Application Delivery to determine the factors that will impact performance before delivering an application or service from the cloud. With real-time information provided by the Cloud Ready Client (i.e. – bandwidth, memory, CPU load, video processing), the webNetwork/SCA Unified Cloud can determine the best delivery method of an application to optimize performance for the end user.

Consider a user that selects to run a spreadsheet from their cloud-based webDesktop. The cloud has several choices of spreadsheet delivery to the end user. The options range from providing a published version, a virtualized version, and web hosted version, or executing the local copy of the spreadsheet. The challenge is determining which delivery method is optimal for the end user. If the user is accessing the cloud through a tablet, then a virtualized or web version of the spreadsheet would be optimal. If the user has a high-end notebook with a spreadsheet installed, they would likely prefer a local copy and just access their data through the cloud. If the user is accessing the spreadsheet application from a friend's house with a poor Internet connection, possibly the web version is the right selection.

The key point is that the performance, and thus the experience, is dependent on many factors such as environment, device, and network bandwidth. webNetwork's ability to determine the optimal delivery method at runtime makes it the first product on the market to truly address performance and cloud computing.

13. Licensing is Easier,

14. Already Have the Server Technology,

15. Already Know How to Do Virtualization

The last three promises can really be bundled together because they all have to do with IT having the expertise, assets and ability to implement a complete solution. Brian did a great job of explaining that having expertise around server virtualization does not automatically mean you have the expertise around VDI. Licensing models around server-based computing can be just as difficult.

webNetwork/SCA's philosophy is to leverage what IT has today and become the stepping stone to the future of web-based applications. Existing directory expertise, servers, imaging tools and network infrastructure can be used successfully to deliver files, applications and reports from the Unified Cloud.

To track licensing, webNetwork/SCA's webManage feature monitors web and application usage to help IT better understand the true application licensing needs.

In Summary

Today, many organizations find themselves struggling to adapt to a rapidly changing computing environment. The challenges of consumerization, BYOD and supporting a wide range of devices are numerous. However, they represent a huge opportunity for IT to not only provide the plumbing but improve ease of use and access to IT services.

Delivering a desktop to a device should no longer be the goal. End users want access to files, applications and data from anywhere and from any device in the simplest way possible.

Before today, you'd probably never heard of the Unified Cloud, so we hope it was interesting and can be useful in helping you meet the challenges facing IT today.

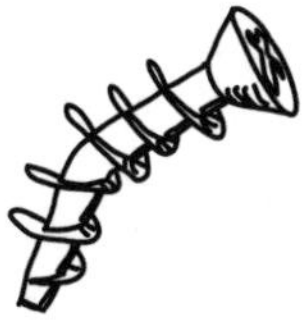